KETO!

RYAN HALL

Copyright © 2020

No part of this publication may be reproduced, distributed, or transmitted in any form or any means, including photocopying, recording, or other electronic or mechanical methods, except as permitted by U.S. copyright law.

Disclaimer

This publication is created to provide information regarding this subject matter. This book is sold with the understanding that the author is not engaged in professional or accurate nutrition advice, but for educational and entertainment purposes only. The author is not liable to any party for any loss, damage, disruption or errors from the content of this book. Before embarking on a new diet or meal plan please consult a professional,

CONTENT

Pesto chops bowl
Pickled Enchiladas
Keto Shrimp Soup
Instant Low Carb Salad
Cauliflower Quesadilla
Scrambled Cheesy Egg
Zucchini Casserole
Coconut Anchovies
Green Smoothie
Garlic Mushrooms
Stuffed Pan Bread
Creamy Asparagus
Naked Beef Burger
Parm Olive Steak
Chicken Bites
Peanut Pudding
Mozzarella Sticks
Grilled Mustard Platter
Loaded Avocados
Creamy Zucchini spaghetti
Avocado sushi
Choco Matcha Crepes
Nut Cookies
Bacon on Spinach
Hasselback zucchini
Cauliflower Tots
Lime Avocados
Cheese Bread Crackers
Bacon Salsa
Beef with Mashed Cauliflower
Keto Hotdogs
Bounty Bars
Low Carb Sandwiches

CONTENT

Almond Smoothie
Vanilla Waffles
Tarragon Frittata
Coconut Cheesecake
Instant Wraps
Cordon bleu Chicken
Greenery egg
Baked Veggies
Baked tomato eggs
Cheese Hash browns
Egg Fajita
Lamb and broccoli
Roasted Platter
Roasted lamb fillets
Beef Parsley Mix
Avocado and prawn cocktail
Pigeon Meal
Prawn coconut curry
Herb Zucchini Omelet
Shrimps with Veggies
Pumpkin spaghetti
Bhaji burger
Pancakes
Kingfish lettuce wraps
Broccoli Mac & cheese
Keto Thai salad
Tomato roasted wings
Spinach fritters with Salsa
Saucy Meatballs with Veggies
Moroccan Chicken
Keto eyeball Spinach
Lemon meringue
Baked Squash with Rice

CONTENT

Baked Bacon Eggs
Avocado Almond Cake
Keto pizza
Keto Cream Puffs
Lemon Delight
Porcini Steak
Tomato Sandwiches
CheeseCake Muffins
Avocado omelet
Stuffed Mushrooms
No-Bake cupcakes
Pork & Cabbage salad
Bacon chips
Keto Hazelnut spread
Cucumber pickle
Keto taco soup
Coated Mozzarella Pearls
Halloumi Spinach
Keto stuffed crepes
Chicken cabbage Dish
Almond gnocchi rolls
Egg tart
Baked eggs
Roasted Salmon
Zucchini Beef Lasagna
Chicken balls
Baked avocado
Coconut bread
Broccoli fritters
Chocolate pudding
Almond butter cookies
Peanut Muffins

What is Keto diet?

Ketogenic diet is the term used for low carbs, high amounts of fat and sufficient protein. Keto diet is like the Atkins Diet. It focuses on the body to burn fats (lose weight) rather than carbohydrates. Keep in mind that you consider those foods which are healthy for your body. You must avoid unhealthy foods like soda, pastries, white bread and sugar. Are you ready to lose weight? "You imagine, You create" don't believe in myths because you'll get confused. Low fat diet doesn't reduce your weight. The best solution is Keto Diet (low carbs), it will help you to lose weight. Don't give up! If you're on a keto diet, it doesn't mean you're totally relying upon this diet. You must do exercise.It may also help you from other diseases such as acne, brain diseases, heart disease and diabetes.

Benefits of Keto Diet

- Lowering your carbs can reduce your appetite and calorie intake.
- Low-carbs help you to lose weight for long term instead of short-term.
- Your abdominal Cavity loses more fat when you're on a low-carb diet.
- Keto diet plays a very effective role to decrease the triglyceride level which increases risk of heart disease.
- It reduces your blood sugar and maintains insulin level.

What makes keto diet so different?

Why is it being so trendy? It basically cuts a huge portion of carbs to its lowest makes a ratio with fats as 4:1.That means 50-60% of fats and only 5-10% of carbs. Rest is compensated with protein

What foods can fulfill the fat requirement of the keto diet?

It's an extremely enjoyable journey! Being a low carb diet, you can never think of having grains like rice, breads and all other whole grain foods. Also No beans and no fruit !

Say yes to butter and creams! Sounds unhealthy? It's not necessary at all. These must be unprocessed and grass fed fats.

In a nutshell, the good fats of the keto-diet make it a healthier and more beneficial diet. Do you know about good fats? All the seeds and nuts are full packages of Omega 3 and Omega 6.Be it flax seeds, almonds or walnuts.

Moreover, chia seeds pudding is mainstream in keto diet. Miraculously delicious! Sesame seeds and olives are introduced as healthy oils. Coconut oil has become a new trend! Who is away from avocado now? A whole complete fat bonus!

Considering meat, fatty fish like salmon or red meat and eggs can be perfect choices to incorporate fatty protein in your diet. What's not can be cooked of all these foods. Hands down to the fascinating and effective keto diet!

PESTO CHOPS BOWL

SERVING: 4 PERSONS
COOKING TIME: 15 MIN

CARBS: 58G
PROTEIN: 186G
FATS: 199G
FIBER: 27G
SODIUM: 1562MG
CALORIES: 2740KCAL

INGREDIENTS

- 1 LB PORK BONELESS CHOPS
- ¼ CUP PESTO SAUCE
- 4 TBSP RICE VINEGAR
- 1 AVOCADO
- ½ CUP PISTACHIOS
- SALT TO TASTE
- PEPPER TO TASTE
- ½ TSP PAPRIKA
- 2 TBSP COCONUT OIL
- 1 DICED TOMATO
- ½ CUP BRINED ASPARAGUS

INSTRUCTIONS

- MARINATE THE CHOPS WITH SALT, PEPPER, AND PESTO SAUCE.
- BLEND THE PISTACHIOS, RICE VINEGAR, PAPRIKA, AND COCONUT OIL IN A BLENDER TO MAKE A SAUCE.
- COOK THE CHOPS FROM BOTH SIDES IN THE OIL FOR 3-4MINUTES PER SIDE.
- CUT THE CHOPS ROUGHLY. PUT THE CHOPS SLICES IN A BOWL. PUT THE SLICED AVOCADOS AND DICED TOMATOES ON IT.
- SPRINKLE BRINED ASPARAGUS ALL OVER. DRIZZLE THE PISTACHIO SAUCE ON IT.

PICKLED ENCHILADAS

SERVING: 4 PERSONS
COOKING TIME: 25 MIN

CARBS: 83G
PROTEIN: 290G
FATS: 233G
FIBER: 23G
SODIUM: 2397MG
CALORIES: 3611KCAL

INGREDIENTS

- 6-8 CABBAGE HEADS
- 2 LB GROUND BEEF
- 1 COARSELY CHOPPED ONION
- 1 TSP GARLIC POWDER
- 2 TBSP ENCHILADAS SAUCE
- 1 TBSP ITALIAN SEASONING
- 1 CUP CHEDDAR CHEESE
- 1 GREEN BELL PEPPER
- 1 RED ONION
- 8-10 BLACK PEPPER PODS
- 1 LIME JUICED
- 1 TBSP VINEGAR
- 2 TBSP COCONUT OIL

INSTRUCTIONS

- SAUTE ONION IN THE OIL. PUT IN BEEF AND GARLIC POWDER IN IT. LET IT COOK FOR 5 MINUTES.
- ADD IN ENCHILADAS SAUCE. COOK A BIT. SEASON IT WITH ITALIAN SEASONING.
- BOIL THE CABBAGE HEADS FOR 2-3 MINUTES IN THE HOT BOILING WATER.
- CUT THE ONION AND BELL PEPPER INTO THICK STRIPS.
- COMBINE LIME JUICE, VINEGAR, BLACK PEPPER PODS IN A JAR. DIP IN ONION AND BELL PEPPER IN IT.
- ADD IN WATER TO DIP THE VEGETABLES COMPLETELY AND LET THEM REST FOR 30-40 MINUTES.
- SPREAD THE CABBAGE HEAD AND STUFF IT WITH BEEF FILLING. THEN ADD THE PICKLED VEGGIES AND WRAP UP THE LEAF TIGHTLY.
- ALIGN THE CABBAGE ENCHILADAS IN THE BAKING DISH. BRUSH THE ENCHILADA SAUCE OVER THE ENCHILADAS.
- SPRINKLE THE CHEESE ON TOP GENEROUSLY.
- BAKE AT 350°F FOR 15 MINUTES. ZERO CARB ENCHILADAS ARE GOOD TO GO!

KETO SHRIMP SOUP

SERVING: 4 PERSONS
COOKING TIME: 25 MIN

CARBS: 72G
PROTEIN: 134G
FATS: 109G
FIBER: 22G
SODIUM: 3533MG
CALORIES: 1733KCAL

INGREDIENTS

- 1 LB SHRIMPS
- 1 CUP COCONUT MILK
- 1 CUP BROTH
- 1 CUP BROCCOLI FLORETS
- 1 DICED LARGE ONION
- 2 MINCED GARLIC CLOVES
- ¼ CUP CHOPPED CORIANDER
- ¼ TSP ROSEMARY
- ¼ CUP ROASTED PEANUTS
- SALT TO TASTE
- PEPPER TO TASTE
- 2 TBSP OLIVE OIL

INSTRUCTIONS

- SEASON THE SHRIMPS WITH SALT AND PEPPER ON BOTH SIDES.
- SEAR THE SHRIMPS UNTIL BROWNED IN OLIVE OIL. TAKE THESE OUT.
- SAUTE THE ONION IN THE SAME PAN ALONG WITH MINCED GARLIC CLOVES.
- DUMP IN BROCCOLI FLORETS AND COOK FOR 1-2 MINUTES.
- POUR IN COCONUT MILK AND BROTH AND LET IT SIMMER FOR 10 MINUTES.
- ADD IN ROASTED PEANUTS AND BLEND THE WHOLE MIXTURE.
- ADD IN SHRIMPS, CORIANDER, AND ROSEMARY AND GIVE IT A GOOD MIX.

GARNISH WITH SOME ROASTED PEANUTS BEFORE SERVING IT!

INSTANT LOW CARB SALAD

SERVING: 2 PERSONS
COOKING TIME: 10 MIN

CARBS: 33G
PROTEIN: 45G
FATS: 85G
FIBER: 15G
SODIUM: 1328MG
CALORIES: 1045KCAL

INGREDIENTS

- 1 CAN WILD TUNA
- ½ CUP MUSHROOMS
- ½ CUP CABBAGE
- ¼ CUP COARSELY CHOPPED ALMONDS
- 2 TBSP GROUND CHIA SEEDS
- ½ CUP CREAM CHEESE
- 2 TBSP MAYONNAISE
- SALT TO TASTE
- PEPPER TO TASTE

INSTRUCTIONS

- CUT THE CABBAGE AND COMBINE IT WITH TUNA AND MUSHROOMS.
- PUT IN CREAM CHEESE AND MAYONNAISE AND MIX IT WELL TO COMBINE EVERYTHING.
- SEASON WITH SALT AND PEPPER AND MIX IT WELL.
- ADD IN COARSELY CHOPPED NUTS AND CHIA SEEDS.

NUTRITIOUS SALAD IS ALL SET!

CAULIFLOWER QUESADILLA

SERVING: 2 PERSONS
COOKING TIME: 15 MIN

CARBS: 65G
PROTEIN: 66G
FATS: 78G
FIBER: 9.4G
SODIUM: 2598MG
CALORIES: 1212KCAL

INGREDIENTS

- 1 CUP CAULIFLOWER RICE
- 1 CUP GRATED CARROT
- 1 CUP GRATED POTATOES
- 2 EGGS
- 4 SMOKED HAM
- 4 CHEESE SLICES
- SALT TO TASTE
- PEPPER TO TASTE
- 1 FRESH THYME STICK
- 2 TBSP AVOCADO OIL

INSTRUCTIONS

- COMBINE THE GRATED CAULIFLOWER, CARROT, AND POTATOES IN A BOWL.
- ADD IN BEATEN EGG, THYME SALT, AND PEPPER AND MAKE IT A BATTER.
- POUR AVOCADO OIL INTO THE PAN AND INVERT THE BATTER TO MAKE A THIN LAYER. LET IT COOK ON LOW FLAME.
- INVERT THE SIDE AFTER 3-4 MINUTES AND THEN ALIGN HAM AND CHEESE SLICES IN IT. LET THE OTHER SIDE COOK FOR 3 MINUTES.
- FOLD IT IN THE SEMI-CIRCLE SHAPE AND CUT IT FROM THE MIDDLE TO MAKE TWO QUARTERS.
- REPEAT THE PROCESS TO MAKE THE OTHER TWO QUARTERS. KEEP UP YOUR KETO GAME WITH CAULIFLOWER QUESADILLAS!

SCRAMBLED CHEESY EGG

SERVING: 2 PERSONS
COOKING TIME: 15 MIN

CARBS: 7.5G
PROTEIN: 40G
FATS: 63G
FIBER: 2.1G
SODIUM: 972MG
CALORIES: 758KCAL

INGREDIENTS

- 4 EGGS
- ¼ CUP CHOPPED PARSLEY
- ¼ CUP SPRING ONION
- ½ CUP SHREDDED CHEESE
- 2 TBSP PITTED OLIVES
- ½ TSP FLAX SEEDS
- 2 TBSP BUTTER

INSTRUCTIONS

- WHISK THE EGGS. MIX UP THE CHOPPED PARSLEY AND SPRING ONION IN THE BEATEN EGG. WHISK IT WELL.
- MELT BUTTER IN THE PAN AND POUR IN THE EGG BATTER. STIR WHILE COOKING FOR ABOUT 3-4 MINUTES.
- TURN OFF THE FLAME AND ADD IN CHEESE AND OLIVES. COVER WITH LID AND LET IT MELT.
- PLATE IT OUT AND SPRINKLE FLAX SEEDS ON IT. HAVE A HEALTHY KETO BREAKFAST!

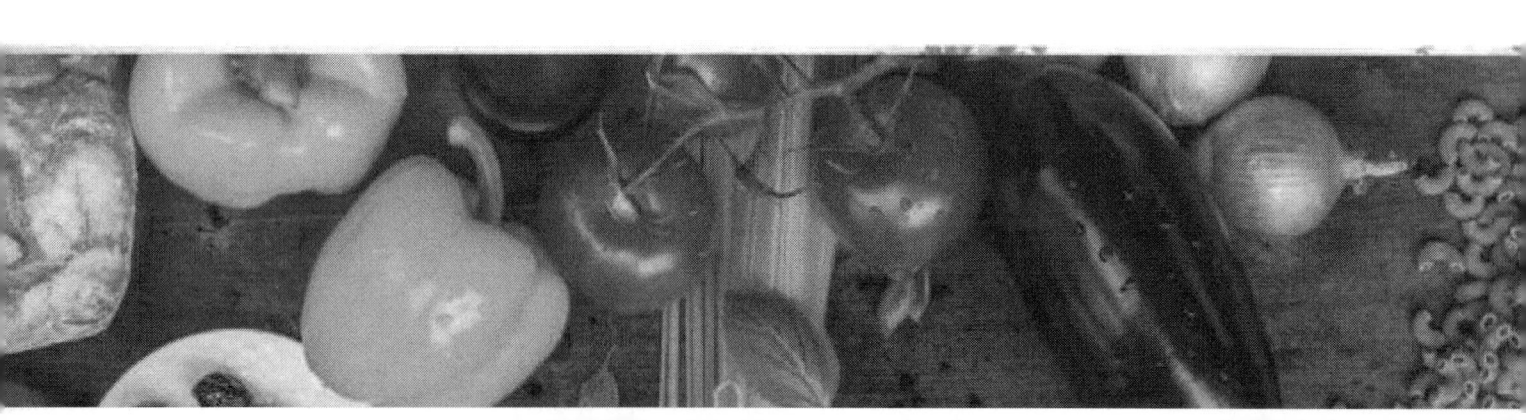

ZUCCHINI CASSEROLE

SERVING: 4 PERSONS
COOKING TIME: 30 MIN

CARBS: 68G
PROTEIN: 192G
FATS: 192G
FIBER: 14G
SODIUM: 3235MG
CALORIES: 2750KCAL

INGREDIENTS

- 2 ZUCCHINIS
- 1 LB BEEF MINCE
- 1 CHOPPED ONION
- 1 TSP GARLIC PASTE
- 4 TBSP TOMATO PASTE
- 1 CUP MOZZARELLA CHEESE
- 1 CUP RICOTTA
- 2 TBSP BUTTER
- ¼ CUP CREAM
- ¼ CUP MILK
- ¼ CUP CHOPPED PARSLEY
- ½ CUP TOMATO SAUCE
- ¼ CUP OLIVES
- ¼ CUP MUSHROOMS
- ¼ TSP CHILI FLAKES
- ¼ TSP OREGANO
- ¼ TSP SESAME SEEDS
- 1 TBSP OLIVE OIL
- SALT TO TASTE
- PEPPER TO TASTE

INSTRUCTIONS

- CUT THE ZUCCHINI INTO LONG THIN SLICES TO MAKE 8-10 SLICES OF A SINGLE ZUCCHINI.
- BOIL THE ZUCCHINI SLICES FOR 5 MINUTES IN THE BOILING WATER.
- SAUTE GARLIC PASTE AND CHOPPED ONION IN OIL AND DUMP TOMATO PASTE AND MINCE IN IT.
- SEASON IT WITH SALT AND PEPPER. LET IT COOK FOR 5-7 MINUTES.
- NOW MELT THE BUTTER IN A PAN AND PUT MILK IN IT. ADD RICOTTA, CREAM, AND PARSLEY. WHISK IT WELL TO MAKE A SMOOTH SAUCE. SEASON IT WITH OREGANO.
- LAYER THE BOILED ZUCCHINI SLICES ON THE BASE OF THE BAKING DISH.
- BRUSH THEM WITH TOMATO SAUCE GENEROUSLY. LAYER THE BEEF ON IT.
- THEN LAYER THE WHITE SAUCE ON IT. PUT IN HALF OF THE MUSHROOMS AND OLIVES ON IT.
- SPRINKLE THE HALF CUP OF CHEESE ON THE TOP. REPEAT THE PROCESS OF LAYERING.
- TOP UP WITH THE LEFTOVER MOZZARELLA CHEESE. SPRINKLE CHILI FLAKES AND SESAME SEEDS FOR THE TOP GARNISHING.
- BAKE AT 350°F FOR 20 MINUTES AND ENJOY THE KETO QUESADILLAS!

COCONUT ANCHOVIES

SERVING: 4 PERSONS
COOKING TIME: 20 MIN

CARBS: 21G
PROTEIN: 142G
FATS: 73G
FIBER: 1.8G
SODIUM: 7536MG
CALORIES: 1337KCAL

INGREDIENTS

- 1 LB ANCHOVIES FILLETS
- 2 TBSP BUTTER
- 1 TSP GARLIC POWDER
- 1 TBSP COCONUT FLOUR
- 1 CUP MILK
- SALT TO TASTE
- BLACK PEPPER TO TASTE
- ¼ TSP WHITE PEPPER

INSTRUCTIONS

- SEASON THE ANCHOVIES WITH SALT AND PEPPER FROM BOTH SIDES.
- GRILL THEM FROM BOTH SIDES TO GET THE TENDER FILLETS.
- START PREPARING THE SAUCE BY MELTING THE BUTTER IN THE PAN.
- ADD IN COCONUT FLOUR AND SAUTE A BIT. THEN ADD MILK AND WHISK WELL.
- ADD GARLIC POWDER AND WHITE PEPPER TO MAKE IT FLAVORFUL. KEEP STIRRING CONSTANTLY.
- POUR THE SAUCE ON THE PLATE AND PLACE THE GRILLED ANCHOVIES IN IT.

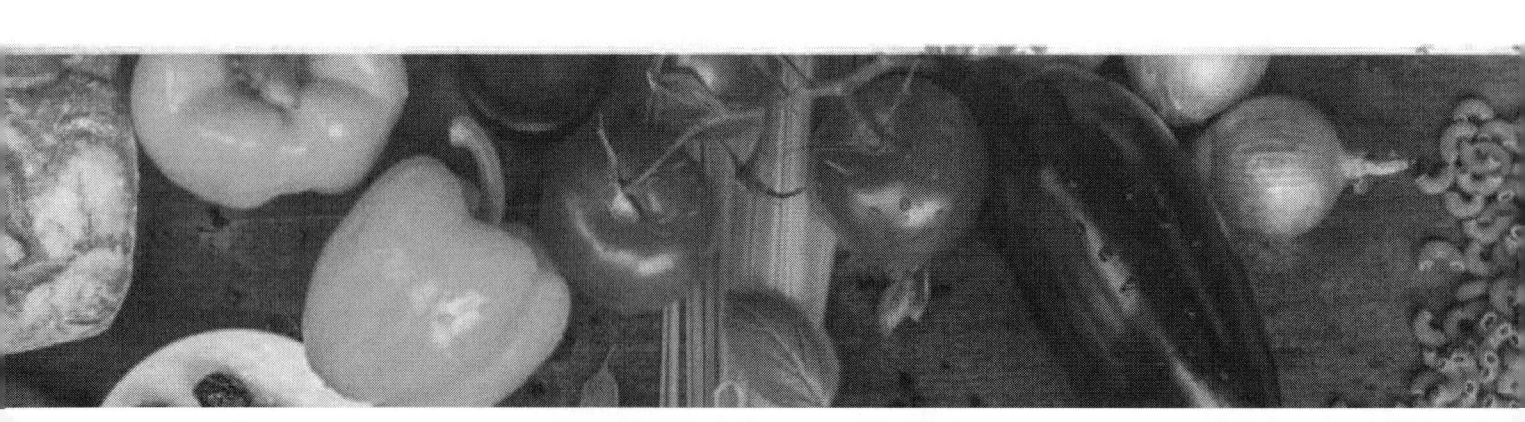

GREEN SMOOTHIE

SERVING: 2 PERSONS
COOKING TIME: 10 MIN

CARBS: 39G
PROTEIN: 14G
FATS: 80G
FIBER: 19G
SODIUM: 339MG
CALORIES: 852KCAL

INGREDIENTS

- ½ CUP BOILED SPINACH
- ½ CUP KALE
- 1 CUCUMBER
- 1 AVOCADO
- 1 TSP FLAX SEEDS
- 1 CUP COCONUT MILK
- ¼ CUP ICE CUBES (OPTIONAL)

INSTRUCTIONS

- BLEND IN ALL THE INGREDIENTS IN THE BLENDER.
- ADD A LOT OF ICE TO MAKE IT COLD, SLUSHY, AND A BIT LIQUID.

HAVE A HEALTHY KETO SMOOTHIE TO START THE DAY!

GARLIC MUSHROOMS

SERVING: 2 PERSONS
COOKING TIME: 25 MIN

CARBS: 28G
PROTEIN: 38G
FATS: 48G
FIBER: 11G
SODIUM: 1429MG
CALORIES: 657KCAL

INGREDIENTS

- 1 CAN MUSHROOMS
- 1 TSP GARLIC POWDER
- ½ CUP PARMESAN
- ½ CUP ALMOND FLOUR
- 1 EGG
- ½ TSP PAPRIKA

INSTRUCTIONS

- COMBINE GARLIC POWDER, PARMESAN, ALMOND FLOUR IN A BOWL.
- CRACK AN EGG IN A BOWL AND BEAT IT WELL WITH PAPRIKA.
- DIP THE MUSHROOMS IN THE BEATEN EGG AND THEN COAT ALL THE MUSHROOMS IN THE FLOUR BATTER GENEROUSLY.
- ALIGN THEM TO THE BAKING TRAY. GIVE IT AN OLIVE OIL SPRAY AND BAKE AT 375°F FOR 18-20 MINUTES.

CRISPY MUSHROOMS ARE GOOD TO EAT!

STUFFED PAN BREAD

SERVING: 4 PERSONS
COOKING TIME: 20 MIN

CARBS: 141G
PROTEIN: 74G
FATS: 182G
FIBER: 30G
SODIUM: 1884MG
CALORIES: 2463KCAL

INGREDIENTS

FOR BREAD
- 1 ½ CUPS COCONUT FLOUR
- ¼ CUP MELTED COCONUT BUTTER
- ¼ CUP OF WATER

FOR STUFFING
- 1 CUP COTTAGE CHEESE
- ½ CUP CREAM CHEESE
- ¼ CUP CHOPPED PARSLEY
- ¼ CUP CHOPPED SPRING ONION
- PINCH OF TURMERIC POWDER
- PINCH OF RED PEPPER POWDER
- ¼ TSP BLACK PEPPER
- ¼ TSP SALT

FOR FRYING
- 4 TBSP AVOCADO OIL

INSTRUCTIONS

- KNEAD THE DOUGH IN THE MIXER BY COMBINING THE BREAD INGREDIENTS. ADJUST THE CONSISTENCY WITH WATER IF NEEDED.
- DUMP IN THE STUFFING INGREDIENTS IN THE BOWL AND MIX EVERYTHING WELL.
- DIVIDE THE DOUGH INTO EQUAL FOUR PARTS. SHAPE UP THE ONE PART INTO A CIRCULAR BREAD.
- PUT IN THE BATTER AND ARRANGE IT ON THE FULL BREAD DOUGH EVENLY.
- FLATTEN ANOTHER PART INTO BREAD AND COVER THE STUFFING.
- SHALLOW FRY IT ON THE PAN IN AVOCADO OIL AND FLIP WHEN COOKED FROM ONE SIDE.
- CUT IT INTO HALF AND ENJOY THE PAN BREAD.

CREAMY ASPARAGUS

SERVING: 1 PERSONS
COOKING TIME: 15 MIN

CARBS: 56G
PROTEIN: 48G
FATS: 100G
FIBER: 13G
SODIUM: 1581MG
CALORIES: 1262KCAL

INGREDIENTS

- 2 CUPS COARSELY CHOPPED ASPARAGUS
- SALT TO TASTE
- PEPPER TO TASTE
- ½ CUP TOMATO PASTE
- 1 CUP CHEESE
- 1 CUP SOUR CREAM
- 1 TBSP OLIVE OIL

INSTRUCTIONS

- TAKE THE ASPARAGUS IN A BOWL. ADD IN SOUR CREAM AND OLIVE OIL.
- SEASON WITH SALT AND PEPPER. MIX IT WELL.
- ADD IN THE TOMATO PASTE AND MIX ASPARAGUS TO COAT IT WELL.
- PUT ALL THE ASPARAGUS IN THE BAKING BOWL AND TOP UP WITH CHEESE GENEROUSLY.
- BAKE IT IN THE PREHEATED OVEN AT 200°C FOR 10-12 MINUTES. ENJOY THE BAKED VEGGIE!

NAKED BEEF BURGER

SERVING: 2 PERSONS
COOKING TIME: 20 MIN

CARBS: 14G
PROTEIN: 66G
FATS: 113G
FIBER: 6.2G
SODIUM: 1134MG
CALORIES: 1332KCAL

INGREDIENTS

- 4 LETTUCE LEAVES
- ½ LB GROUND BEEF
- ¼ CUP CHOPPED CAPSICUM
- ¼ CUP CHOPPED OLIVES
- 1 TBSP DRIED PARSLEY
- 4 TBSP GARLIC MAYO
- 2 TBSP AVOCADO OIL

INSTRUCTIONS

- COMBINE THE GROUND BEEF, CHOPPED CAPSICUM, PARSLEY, AND OLIVES IN A BOWL.
- SHAPE UP THE TWO PATTIES OUT OF THE BATTER. FRY IN OLIVE OIL FOR AROUND 10 MINUTES.
- FLATTEN THE LETTUCE LEAF AND PLACE PATTIE ON IT. POUR IN GARLIC MAYO ON IT. COVER WITH ANOTHER LEAF.
- REPEAT THE PROCESS TO MAKE UP THE SECOND NAKED BURGER.

EAT A DELICIOUS BURGER WITH A KETO DIET!

PARM OLIVE STEAK

SERVING: 4 PERSONS
COOKING TIME: 20 MIN

CARBS: 72G
PROTEIN: 158G
FATS: 156G
FIBER: 14G
SODIUM: 4548MG
CALORIES: 2343KCAL

INGREDIENTS

- 1 LB BEEF STEAK
- 1 TBSP GINGER GARLIC PASTE
- 1 CUP PARMESAN
- 1/2 CUP MARINARA SAUCE
- ¼ CUP COCONUT MILK
- ½ CUP BLACK OLIVES
- SALT TO TASTE
- PEPPER TO TASTE
- ½ TSP THYME
- ½ TSP FIVE-SPICE POWDER
- ½ TSP GREEN CHILI PASTE
- 1 TBSP TACO SEASONING
- 1 TBSP BUTTER

INSTRUCTIONS

- COMBINE SALT, PEPPER, THYME, FIVE-SPICE POWDER, AND GREEN CHILI PASTE.
- FOLD THE STEAKS IN THESE SPICES AND LET IT REST FOR 10-15 MINUTES.
- GRILL THE STEAKS ON THE GRILLER PAN FROM BOTH SIDES TO GET THE TEMPTING MARKS.
- PREPARE THE SAUCE BY SAUTEING GINGER GARLIC PASTE IN THE MELTED BUTTER.
- POUR IN MARINARA SAUCE, COCONUT MILK, AND ADD IN SALT AND PEPPER. WHISK IT WELL.
- ADD IN PARMESAN, TACO SEASONING, AND MIX IT WELL. DUMP IN OLIVES IN THE END.
- POUR IN HOT SAUCE OVER THE GRILLED STEAK AND SERVE HOT.

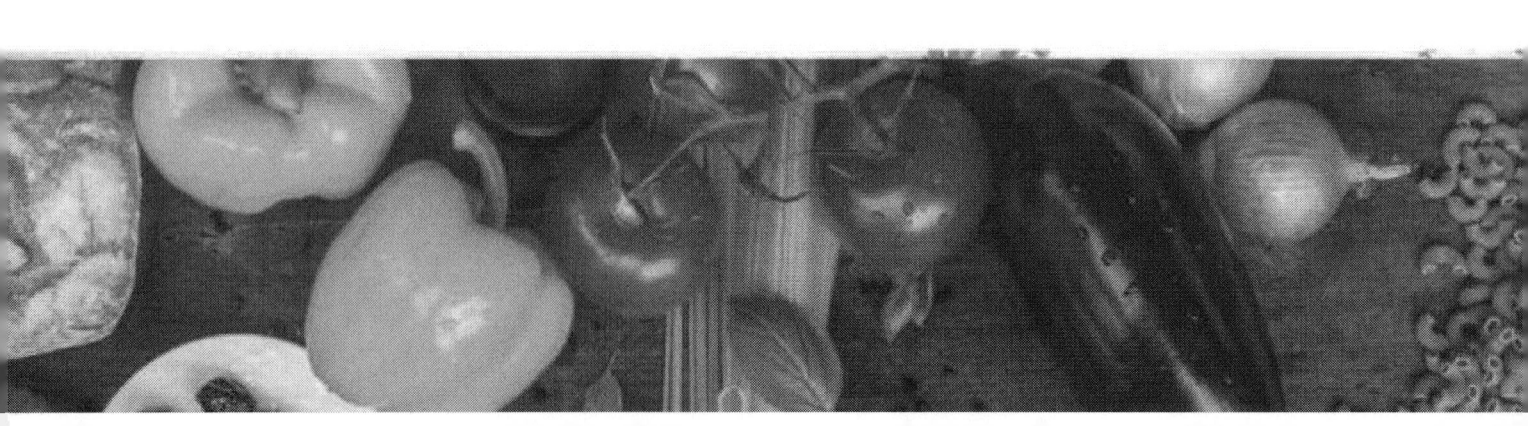

CHICKEN BITES

SERVING: 4 PERSONS
COOKING TIME: 30 MIN

CARBS: 51G
PROTEIN: 118G
FATS: 130G
FIBER: 19G
SODIUM: 2703MG
CALORIES: 1787KCAL

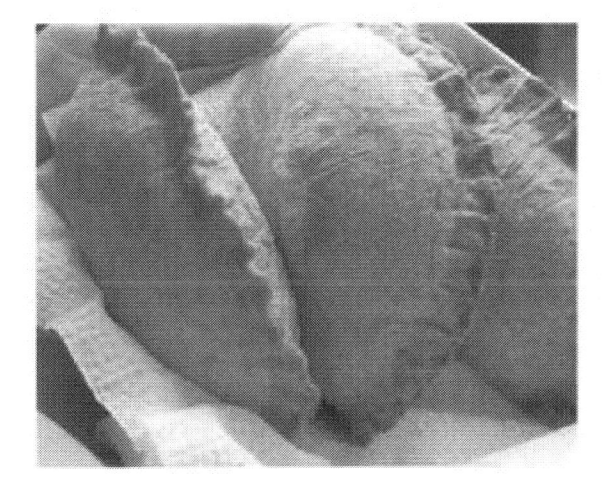

INGREDIENTS

- ½ LB CHICKEN MINCE
- ½ CUP CHOPPED CELERY
- ½ CUP CHOPPED SPINACH
- SALT TO TASTE
- PEPPER TO TASTE
- ½ TSP OREGANO
- 1 TBSP SOY SAUCE
- ½ TSP GARLIC POWDER
- 1 CUP SHREDDED CHEESE
- 1 CUP ALMOND FLOUR
- ¾ CUP YOGURT
- 2 TBSP CREAM CHEESE

INSTRUCTIONS

- COMBINE ALMOND FLOUR, YOGURT, AND CREAM CHEESE IN A BOWL.
- MIX UP WELL TO FORM THE DOUGH.
- COMBINE MINCE, CELERY, AND SPINACH, CHEESE, AND DUMP IN ALL THE SEASONINGS. MIX WELL TO FORM THE BATTER.
- FLATTEN THE DOUGH AND CUT INTO CIRCULAR SHAPES.
- STUFF IN THE CHICKEN BATTER AND FOLD TO MAKE EMPANADAS. YOU CAN CHOOSE DIFFERENT SHAPES. SEAL THE ENDS WITH THE FORK.
- MAKE 8-10 EMPANADAS OUT OF IT.
- BAKE IN THE PREHEATED OVEN AT 180°C FOR 15-18 MINUTES.

PEANUT PUDDING

SERVING: 3 PERSONS
COOKING TIME: 10 MIN

CARBS: 45G
PROTEIN: 37G
FATS: 122G
FIBER: 11G
SODIUM: 459MG
CALORIES: 1352KCAL

INGREDIENTS

- ¾ CUP YOGURT
- ½ CUP CREAM
- 4 TBSP PEANUT BUTTER
- 2 TSP CHIA SEEDS
- 2 TBSP ZERO CARB SWEETENER
- ¼ CUP ROUGHLY CHOPPED WALNUTS
- ¼ CUP ROUGHLY CHOPPED BRAZIL NUTS

INSTRUCTIONS

- DIP THE CHIA SEEDS IN A QUARTER CUP OF WATER AND LET IT REST FOR 5-10 MINUTES.
- WHISK THE CREAM AND YOGURT IN A BOWL.
- ADD IN SWEETENER, PEANUT BUTTER, AND CHOPPED NUTS.
- MIX THE BATTER WELL. AND ADD IN CHIA SEEDS ONCE THEY ARE PROOF.
- POUR OUT IN THE DESSERT GLASSES AND LET IT COOL FOR 4-5 HOURS.

YOU DON'T HAVE TO SKIP DESSERT ON KETO!

MOZZARELLA STICKS

SERVING: 2 PERSONS
COOKING TIME: 15 MIN

CARBS: 27G
PROTEIN: 45G
FATS: 181G
FIBER: 15G
SODIUM: 464MG
CALORIES: 1855KCAL

INGREDIENTS

- 1 MOZZARELLA BLOCK
- 1 CUP ALMOND FLOUR
- 1 TSP OREGANO
- 1 TSP DRIED PARSLEY
- PINCH OF SALT
- 1 TBSP CHICKEN POWDER
- 2 EGGS
- ½ CUP OLIVE OIL

INSTRUCTIONS

- DUMP ALL THE DRY INGREDIENTS IN A BOWL AND MIX THEM WELL.
- CRACK EGGS IN A BOWL AND BEAT THEM WELL.
- CUT THE MOZZARELLA BLOCK INTO THICK LONG STICKS.
- DIP THE STICKS IN THE BEATEN EGG AND THEN FOLD IN ALMOND FLOUR.
- FRY THE STICKS IN THE OLIVE OIL AND GET THE GOLDEN CRUNCHY CHEESE STICKS.

GRILLED MUSTARD PLATTER

SERVING: 2 PERSONS
COOKING TIME: 25 MIN

CARBS: 26G
PROTEIN: 146G
FATS: 56G
FIBER: 7G
SODIUM: 1774MG
CALORIES: 1208KCAL

INGREDIENTS

- 1 LB CHICKEN BREASTS
- 2 TSP MUSTARD PASTE
- 4 MINCED GARLIC CLOVES
- 1 TSP BASIL LEAVES
- SALT TO TASTE
- PEPPER TO TASTE
- ½ CUP ONION RINGS
- ½ CUP COARSELY CHOPPED ASPARAGUS
- ¼ CUP DICED TOMATOES
- ½ CUP BLACK OLIVES
- 2 TBSP OLIVE OIL

INSTRUCTIONS

- CUT THE CHICKEN BREAST INTO THIN FILLETS.
- MARINATE THE FILLETS WITH SALT, PEPPER, MUSTARD PASTE, GARLIC, AND BASIL LEAVES.
- LET IT REST FOR 10 MINUTES AND HEAT OIL ON THE GRILL PAN.
- GRILL EACH SIDE OF THE FILLET FOR 5 MINUTES. BRUSH THE LEFTOVER MARINADE ON THE FILLETS.
- TAKE OUT THE FILLETS AND GRILL ONION RINGS, TOMATOES, OLIVES, AND ASPARAGUS ON THE SAME PAN.
- SPREAD THE VEGGIES ON THE GRILLED CHICKEN FILLETS AND EAT A COMPLETE HEALTHY MEAL!

LOADED AVOCADOS

SERVING: 2 PERSONS
COOKING TIME: 15 MIN

CARBS: 63G
PROTEIN: 40G
FATS: 143G
FIBER: 21G
SODIUM: 2215MG
CALORIES: 1667KCAL

INGREDIENTS

- 1 AVOCADO
- 2 SAUSAGES
- ½ TBSP SRIRACHA SAUCE
- 1 TBSP TOMATO PASTE
- 1 TSP GARLIC PASTE
- ½ CUP COCONUT FLOUR
- 1 EGG
- 4 TBSP AVOCADO OIL
- SALT TO TASTE
- PEPPER TO TASTE

INSTRUCTIONS

- CUT THE AVOCADO INTO STRIPS.
- MIX IN SALT AND PEPPER IN THE ALMOND FLOUR.
- DIP AVOCADO STIPS IN THE EGG AND THEN FOLD IN THE ALMOND FLOUR.
- ARRANGE THE AVOCADOS IN THE BAKING TRAY. BAKE THEM FOR 10-12 MINUTES AT 375°F.
- PREPARE THE SAUCE BY COMBINING SRIRACHA SAUCE, TOMATO PASTE AND GARLIC PASTE IN A BOWL.
- POUR IN THE SAUCE INTO THE PAN AND CUT THE SAUSAGES INTO IT. LET IT SIMMER FOR 1 MINUTE.
- DRIZZLE THE SAUCE ALL OVER THE AVOCADOS AND GET THE SPICY AVOCADOS.

CREAMY ZUCCHINI SPAGHETTI

SERVING: 2 PERSONS
COOKING TIME: 15 MIN

CARBS: 27G
PROTEIN: 14G
FATS: 116G
FIBER: 8.1G
SODIUM: 672MG
CALORIES: 1161KCAL

INGREDIENTS

- 2 ZUCCHINIS
- 1 CUP CREAM
- 2 MINCED CLOVES
- SALT TO TASTE
- BLACK PEPPER TO TASTE
- ½ CUP CHOPPED ARCHIVES
- ½ CUP MUSHROOMS
- 2 TBSP AVOCADO OIL

INSTRUCTIONS

- SPIRALIZE THE ZUCCHINI INTO ZUCCHINI NOODLES.
- MELT THE BUTTER IN THE PAN AND SAUTE GARLIC IN IT.
- POUR IN THE CREAM AND ADD THE NOODLES AND SEASON IT WITH SALT AND PEPPER.
- ADD IN CHOPPED ARCHIVES AND MUSHROOMS AND LET THE CREAM SIMMER FOR 1-2 MINUTES.

INSTANT LOW CARB NOODLES ARE READY TO SERVE!

AVOCADO SUSHI

SERVING: 2 PERSONS
COOKING TIME: 15 MIN

CARBS: 35G
PROTEIN: 56G
FATS: 95G
FIBER: 13G
SODIUM: 2009MG
CALORIES: 1196KCAL

INGREDIENTS

- 1 CUP BOILED BROCCOLI FLORETS
- 6 OZ CREAM CHEESE
- 1 TBSP SRIRACHA SAUCE
- 1 TBSP SOY SAUCE
- 6 OZ SALMON STRIPS
- ½ AVOCADO
- 2 BOILED ASPARAGUS STICKS
- 2 NORI SHEETS

INSTRUCTIONS

- GRATE THE BROCCOLI HEAD INTO BROCCOLI RICE.
- MIX UP THE CREAM CHEESE, SOY SAUCE, AND SRIRACHA SAUCE WITH BROCCOLI RICE AND MIX IT THOROUGHLY TO MAKE A BATTER.
- CUT THE AVOCADOS INTO THIN FLAT SLICES.
- SPREAD THE NORI SHEET AND SPREAD HALF OF THE BROCCOLI BATTER.
- CUT THE ASPARAGUS INTO HALF AND ALIGN IN THE MIDDLE ON THE RICE VERTICALLY.
- ALIGN THE SALMON STRIPS IN THE MIDDLE AND ROLL UP THE NORI SHEET.

CUT INTO HALF AND ENJOY THE LOW CARB SUSHI!

CHOCO MATCHA CREPES

SERVING: 2 PERSONS
COOKING TIME: 15 MIN

CARBS: 72G
PROTEIN: 29G
FATS: 170G
FIBER: 4.8G
SODIUM: 476MG
CALORIES: 1894KCAL

INGREDIENTS

- 2 EGGS
- 2 TBSP CREAM CHEESE
- ½ CUP ALMOND MILK
- ¼ CUP SUGAR-FREE COCOA POWDER
- ¼ CUP ALMOND FLOUR
- 1 TBSP MATCHA (GREEN TEA POWDER)
- 2 TBSP MELTED BUTTER
- 2 TBSP COCONUT OIL
- 1 CUP HEAVY CREAM

INSTRUCTIONS

- BLEND THE EGGS, CREAM CHEESE, ALMOND MILK IN A BLENDER.
- DUMP IN MELTED BUTTER AND BLEND IT WELL.
- COMBINE ALMOND FLOUR, COCOA POWDER IN A BOWL. ADD IN 1 TBSP OF MATCHA TO IT.
- DUMP IN THESE DRY INGREDIENTS IN A BLENDER AND LET IT BLEND ALL THE BATTER NICELY.
- MELT IN A TABLESPOON OF BUTTER AND POUR IN A BATTER TO MAKE A THIN LAYER OF CREPE.
- ONCE DONE, FLIP THE SIDE AND COOK FOR 1-2 MINUTES ON EACH SIDE.
- WHIP UP THE CREAM AND ADD IN LEFTOVER MATCHA TO IT.
- SERVE THE CREPES WITH THIS MATCHA CREAM OR STUFF CREPES WITH IT AND ROLL THEM UP. DRIZZLE THE SUGAR-FREE MELTED CHOCOLATE ALL OVER THE CREPES.

NUT COOKIES

SERVING: 2 PERSONS
COOKING TIME: 15 MIN

CARBS: 28G
PROTEIN: 25G
FATS: 63G
FIBER: 13G
SODIUM: 94MG
CALORIES: 744KCAL

INGREDIENTS

- 4 TBSP ALMOND FLOUR
- 4 TBSP ALMOND BUTTER
- 1 TBSP CHOPPED ALMONDS
- 1 TBSP CHOPPED PISTACHIOS
- SUGAR-FREE CHOCOLATE CHIPS
- DROPS OF VANILLA ESSENCE
- 2 TBSP MILK

INSTRUCTIONS

- MIX UP ALMOND FLOUR, COCONUT FLOUR IN A BOWL.
- ADD IN BUTTER KEPT AT ROOM TEMPERATURE AND MIX IN THE BATTER.
- COMBINE THE BUTTER WITH FINGERS.
- NOW ADD VANILLA ESSENCE, CRUSHED NUTS, MILK, AND CHOCOLATE CHIPS AND MIX GENTLY.
- SHAPE UP THE COOKIES OUT OF THE BATTER. SPRINKLE SOME NUTS ON THE TOP.
- POP IN THE PREHEATED OVEN AT 350°F FOR 10-12 MINUTES.

MAKE A COMBO OF EVENING COFFEE WITH KETO COOKIES!

BACON ON SPINACH

SERVING: 2 PERSONS
COOKING TIME: 30 MIN

CARBS: 41G
PROTEIN: 61G
FATS: 100G
FIBER: 18G
SODIUM: 2779MG
CALORIES: 1266KCAL

INGREDIENTS

- 2 CUPS SPINACH LEAVES
- 8-10 BACONS
- ½ TSP SALT
- ¼ CUP MILK
- 2 TBSP COCONUT BUTTER
- 2 MINCED GARLIC CLOVES
- 1 TSP RED CHILI PASTE
- 2 TBSP CREAM CHEESE

INSTRUCTIONS

- MELT THE BUTTER IN THE PAN. ADD IN SPINACH LEAVES AND SEASON THEM WITH SALT. LET IT COOK UNTIL THEY SHRINK A BIT.
- WHEN SHRANK AFTER 10-12 MINUTES, PUT IN MINCED GARLIC, AND COOK.
- POUR IN MILK AND LET THEM COOK FOR MORE THAN 5-10 MINUTES.
- BRUSH THE BACON WITH RED CHILI PASTE SLIGHTLY AND CRISP THEM IN THE LEFTOVER BUTTER ON THE PAN.
- ARRANGE THE SPINACH LEAVES ON THE PLATTER. PLACE BACON ON IT AND SERVE WITH CREAM CHEESE.

HASSELBACK ZUCCHINI

SERVING: 2 PERSONS
COOKING TIME: 30 MIN

CARBS: 34G
PROTEIN: 73G
FATS: 107G
FIBER: 7.7G
SODIUM: 2579MG
CALORIES: 1380KCAL

INGREDIENTS

- 2 ZUCCHINI
- 1 TBSP GARLIC POWDER
- 2 TSP ONION POWDER
- 2 TBSP OLIVE OIL
- SALT TO TASTE
- PEPPER TO TASTE
- 10 BACON STRIPS
- 1 TBSP TACO SEASONING
- 1 CUP SHREDDED CHEESE

INSTRUCTIONS

- CUT THE SLITS IN THE ZUCCHINI MAKING IT HASSELBACK.
- DRIZZLE OLIVE OIL ON IT. CUT THE BACON STRIPS INTO HALVES. ARRANGE THE BACON SLICES IN THE ALTERNATIVE SLITS.
- SPRINKLE ONION POWDER, GARLIC POWDER, SALT, PEPPER, AND TACO SEASONING ON IT.
- SPREAD IT EVENLY ON THE ZUCCHINI. SPREAD CHEESE ALL OVER IT.
- BAKE AT 400°F FOR 25 MINUTES.

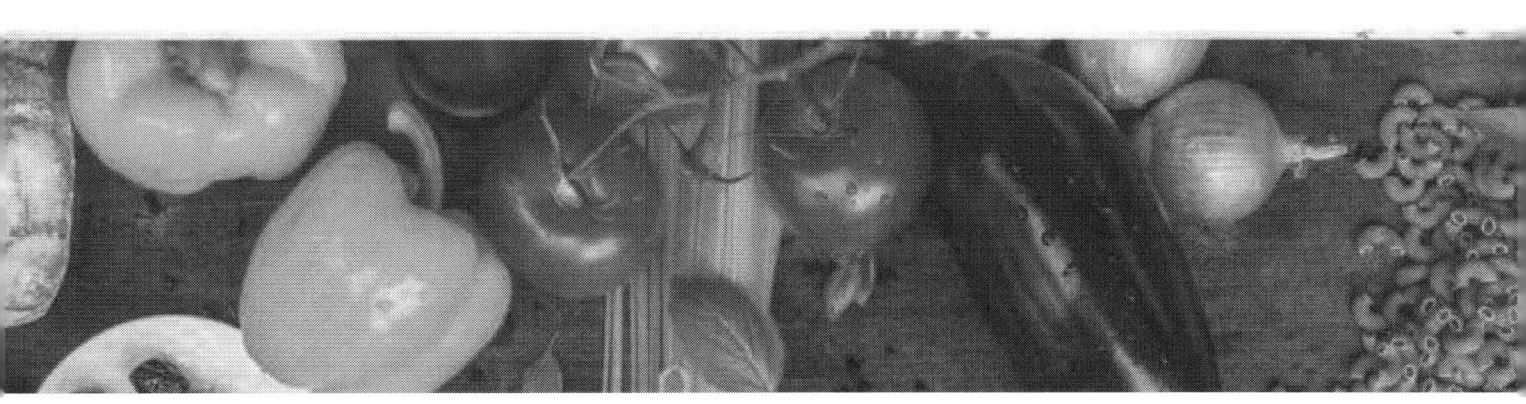

CAULIFLOWER TOTS

SERVING: 2 PERSONS
COOKING TIME: 30 MIN

CARBS: 31G
PROTEIN: 50G
FATS: 72G
FIBER: 14G
SODIUM: 1434MG
CALORIES: 931KCAL

INGREDIENTS

- 2 CUP CHOPPED CAULIFLOWER
- ½ TSP LEMON ZEST
- 1 TSP GARLIC POWDER
- 1 CUP GRATED CHEESE
- ½ CUP ALMOND FLOUR
- ½ CUP CHOPPED MINT LEAVES
- SALT TO TASTE
- BLACK PEPPER TO TASTE
- 2 EGGS

INSTRUCTIONS

- COMBINE THE GRATED CAULIFLOWER, CHOPPED MINT LEAVES, CHEESE IN A BOWL.
- MIX THEM WELL. ADD LEMON ZEST TO IT.
- SEASON IT WITH GARLIC POWDER, SALT, AND PEPPER. MIX UP THE BATTER.
- SHAPE UP THE SMALL TOTS FROM THE BATTER AND DIP IT IN THE BEATEN EGGS.
- BAKE IN THE PREHEATED OVEN AT 400°F FOR 10 MINUTES.
- FLIP THE SIDE AFTER 10 MINUTES AND LET IT COOK FOR ANOTHER 10 MINUTES.

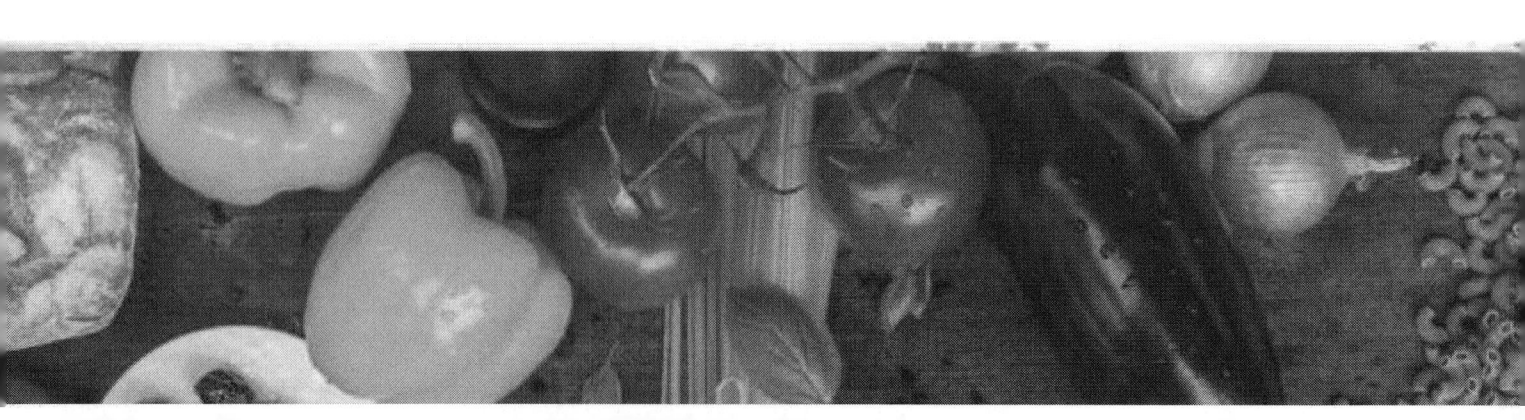

LIME AVOCADOS

SERVING: 2 PERSONS
COOKING TIME: 15 MIN

CARBS: 52G
PROTEIN: 68G
FATS: 119G
FIBER: 29G
SODIUM: 2009MG
CALORIES: 1497KCAL

INGREDIENTS

- 2 AVOCADOS
- 1 CAN TUNA
- ½ CUP PARMESAN
- ½ TSP GARLIC POWDER
- ½ CUP CHOPPED TOMATOES
- ½ CUP CHOPPED CELERY
- ¼ CUP CREAM CHEESE
- 2 TBSP MAYONNAISE

INSTRUCTIONS

- COMBINE THE TUNA, TOMATOES, AND CELERY IN A BOWL.
- SEASON IT WITH GARLIC POWDER, SALT, AND BLACK PEPPER. PUT IN PARMESAN AS WELL.
- NOW DUMP IN CREAM CHEESE AND MAYO AND MIX IT WELL.
- CUT THE AVOCADO INTO HALVES AND REMOVE THE SEED.
- STUFF IN THE TUNA BATTER AND BAKE IT AT 375°F FOR 10 MINUTES.

CHEESE BREAD CRACKERS

SERVING: 2 PERSONS
COOKING TIME: 25 MIN

CARBS: 37G
PROTEIN: 55G
FATS: 101G
FIBER: 8.9G
SODIUM: 2839MG
CALORIES: 1240KCAL

INGREDIENTS

- 1 EGG
- ½ CUP CREAM CHEESE
- 1 CUP PARMESAN
- ½ CUP ALMOND FLOUR
- ½ CUP CHOPPED PARSLEY
- SALT TO TASTE
- PEPPER TO TASTE
- ½ TSP OREGANO

INSTRUCTIONS

- PUT IN FLOUR, PARMESAN, AND PARSLEY IN THE BOWL.
- PUT EGG, CREAM CHEESE IN IT. SEASON IT WITH SALT, PEPPER, AND OREGANO.
- GIVE IT A GOOD MIX TO MAKE THE DOUGH.
- FLATTEN THE DOUGH IN THE BAKING TRAY AT 350°F FOR 12-15 MINUTES.
- ONE DONE, CUT INTO CRACKERS AND ENJOY THE KETO CRISPS.

BACON SALSA

SERVING: 2 PERSONS
COOKING TIME: 15 MIN

CARBS: 31G
PROTEIN: 37G
FATS: 57G
FIBER: 6.2G
SODIUM: 2337MG
CALORIES: 767KCAL

INGREDIENTS

- 8 BACON STRIPS
- ¼ CUP RED BELL PEPPER
- ¼ CUP YELLOW BELL PEPPER
- 1 DICED ONION
- ½ CUP CUBED ICEBERG
- 1 CUCUMBER
- ½ CUP MUSHROOMS
- 1 TBSP LEMON JUICE
- 1 TSP PUMPKIN SEEDS
- ¼ TSP RED CHILI FLAKES
- SALT TO TASTE
- PEPPER TO TASTE
- 2 TBSP BUTTER

INSTRUCTIONS

- MELT THE BUTTER IN THE PAN AND CRISP THE BACON STRIPS IN IT FOR ABOUT 5-7 MINUTES.
- CUT THE STRIPS INTO PIECES AND ADD THEM TO A BOWL.
- DICE THE RED BELL PEPPER, YELLOW BELL PEPPER, CUCUMBER, ONION, AND MUSHROOMS. CUT THE ICEBERG CUBES.
- DUMP IN THESE VEGGIES IN THE BACON. MIX IT WELL.
- PUT IN SEEDS. ADD IN THE SEASONINGS. AND TOSS EVERYTHING NICELY.

QUICK SALSA IS READY WITH A FUSION OF FLAVORS!

BEEF WITH MASHED CAULIFLOWER

SERVING: 2 PERSONS
COOKING TIME: 25 MIN

CARBS: 38G
PROTEIN: 145G
FATS: 134G
FIBER: 9.1G
SODIUM: 1550MG
CALORIES: 1978KCAL

INGREDIENTS

- 1 LB BEEF MINCE
- ½ CUP TOMATO PASTE
- DASH OF RED CHILI FLAKES
- 1 TSP GINGER GARLIC PASTE
- 1 CUP CAULIFLOWER FLORETS
- ¼ CUP SOUR CREAM
- ½ CUP MOZZARELLA CHEESE
- SALT TO TASTE
- PEPPER TO TASTE
- 1 TBSP CHOPPED PARSLEY
- 2 TBSP AVOCADO OIL

INSTRUCTIONS

- HEAT THE AVOCADO OIL IN THE PAN AND SAUTE GINGER GARLIC PASTE.
- DUMP IN THE MINCED BEEF AND LET IT COOK A BIT FOR 3-4 MINUTES.
- NOW ADD TOMATO PASTE AND CHILI FLAKES TO IT.
- LET IT COOK FOR 5-6 MINUTES UNTIL THE GRAVY BECOMES THICK.
- BOIL THE CAULIFLOWER IN THE BOILING WATER FOR 5-6 MINUTES UNTIL IT BECOMES SOFT
- WHEN DRAINED, ADD SOUR CREAM, CHEESE, SALT, AND PEPPER TO IT. MASH THE WHOLE MIXTURE.
- SPRINKLE PARSLEY ON THE TOP. SERVE WITH THE FLAVORFUL BEEF!

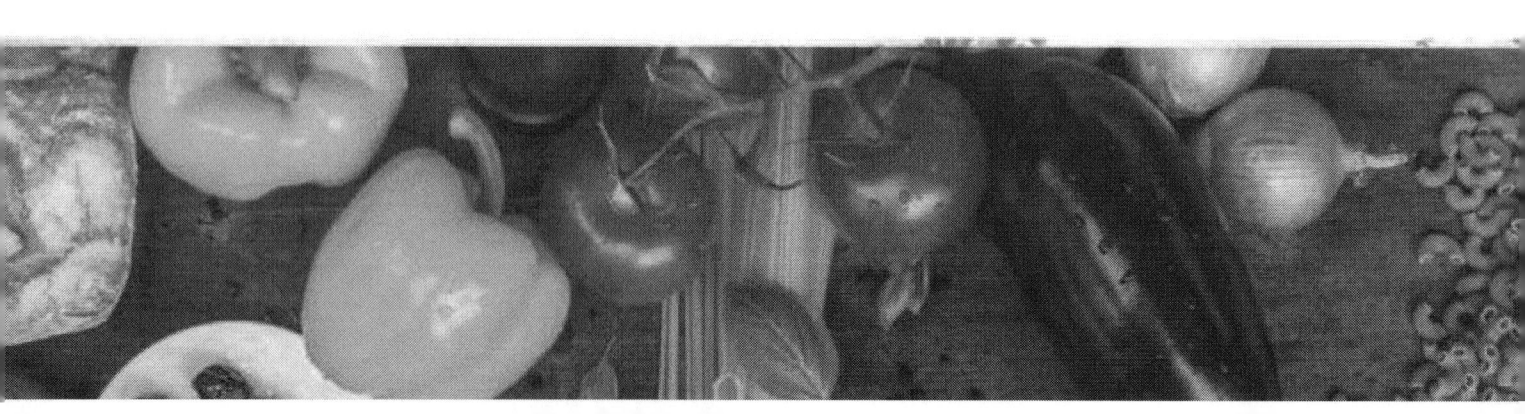

KETO HOTDOGS

SERVING: 2 PERSONS
COOKING TIME: 25 MIN

CARBS: 95G
PROTEIN: 85G
FATS: 226G
FIBER: 14G
SODIUM: 3253MG
CALORIES: 2739KCAL

INGREDIENTS

FOR BREAD
- 1 CUP COCONUT FLOUR
- 1 CUP PARMESAN
- ½ CUP MELTED BUTTER
- ¼ TSP SALT
- ½ TSP PEPPER
- 1 TSP BAKING POWDER
- ½ TSP THYME
- 2 EGGS
- 1 TBSP OLIVE OIL

FOR FILLING
- 2 SAUSAGES
- 2 TBSP MAYONNAISE
- ½ TSP SRIRACHA SAUCE
- 1 TSP MUSTARD PASTE
- 2 ICEBERG LEAVES

INSTRUCTIONS

- COMBINE ALL THE DRY INGREDIENTS OF BREAD IN A BOWL.
- THEN ADD IN MELTED BUTTER AND BEATEN EGGS. MIX THE BATTER WELL.
- SPREAD THE BATTER IN THE BUTTER PAPER ALIGNED RECTANGULAR BAKING DISH. BAKE IT AT 375°F FOR 5-8 MINUTES.
- ONCE DONE, CUT FROM THE CROSS-SECTIONAL CENTER AND DIVIDE IT INTO TWO PIECES OF BREAD. NOW CUT FROM THE CENTER TO DIVIDE INTO FOUR.
- NOW CUT THE SAUSAGES INTO MINI SLICES. AND SAUTE A BIT ON THE PAN IN OLIVE OIL TO COOK THEM.
- MAKE A SAUCE BY COMBINING MAYONNAISE, SRIRACHA SAUCE, AND MUSTARD PASTE IN A BOWL.
- ALIGN ICEBERG ON THE BASE OF THE BREAD. THEN ARRANGE SAUSAGES AND DRIZZLE A LOT OF SAUCE AND COVER WITH ANOTHER BREAD.
- REPEAT THE PROCESS FOR THE SECOND HOTDOG.

NO NEED TO CRAVE ANYMORE!

BOUNTY BARS

SERVING: 4 PERSONS
COOKING TIME: 10 MIN

CARBS: 179G
PROTEIN: 47G
FATS: 217G
FIBER: 30G
SODIUM: 640MG
CALORIES: 2766KCAL

INGREDIENTS

- 4 TBSP COCONUT BUTTER
- 4 TBSP PEANUT BUTTER
- ½ CUP CREAM
- ¼ CUP FINELY CHOPPED PECANS
- ¼ CUP COCONUT FLOUR
- 1 TSP GROUND HEMP SEEDS
- ½ CUP COCONUT FLAKES
- 1 CUP ZERO CARB CHOCOLATE
- ¼ CUP COCONUT MILK

INSTRUCTIONS

- MELT THE PEANUT BUTTER IN A BOWL. MIX UP COCONUT BUTTER, PEANUT BUTTER, AND HEAVY CREAM IN A BOWL.
- PUT IN THE COCONUT FLOUR AND MIX EVERYTHING NICELY.
- DUMP IN HALF OF THE COCONUT FLAKES, HEMP SEEDS, AND NUTS IN THE BUTTER BATTER.
- LAYER THIS BATTER IN THE DISH AND CHILL IT FOR 3-4 HOURS.
- MELT THE CHOCOLATE WITH COCONUT MILK FOR A MINUTE IN THE MICROWAVE.
- AFTER THE CREAM LAYER GETS A BIT FIRM, LAYER MELTED CHOCOLATE ON IT.
- SPRINKLE LEFTOVER COCONUT FLAKES ON THE TOP. AGAIN PLACE IT IN THE REFRIGERATOR AND CUT THEM INTO BARS WHEN CHILLED.

GRAB IT FROM THE REFRIGERATOR WHENEVER YOU FEEL LOW!

LOW CARB SANDWICHES

SERVING: 1 PERSONS
COOKING TIME: 10 MIN

CARBS: 28G
PROTEIN: 65G
FATS: 62G
FIBER: 2.3G
SODIUM: 1860MG
CALORIES: 745KCAL

INSTRUCTIONS

- PREPARE THE FRESH KETO WAFFLES. MAKE SURE TO KEEP THEM A LITTLE THICK.
- SPREAD GARLIC MAYO AND THEN LAYER ICEBERG, CHEESE SLICE, HAMS, AND JALAPENOS WITH THE SEQUENCE.
- DRIZZLE THE GARLIC MAYO AGAIN AND COVER WITH ANOTHER WAFFLE.

THIS SANDWICH IS A FOREVER YAY!

INGREDIENTS

- 2 WAFFLES
- 1 CHEESE SLICE
- 1 ICEBERG LEAF
- 3 HAMS
- 3-4 JALAPENOS SLICES
- 2 TBSP GARLIC MAYO

ALMOND SMOOTHIE

SERVING: 2 PERSONS
COOKING TIME: 5 MIN

CARBS: 31G
PROTEIN: 27G
FATS: 85G
FIBER: 7.8G
SODIUM: 517MG
CALORIES: 759KCAL

INGREDIENTS

- 1 CUP MILK
- ½ CUP CREAM
- ½ CUP CRUSHED ALMONDS
- 1 TSP ALMOND ESSENCE

INSTRUCTIONS

- BLEND MILK AND CRUSHED ALMONDS IN THE BLENDER.
- THEN ADD CREAM, AND ESSENCE AND BLEND IT WELL.
- YOU CAN ADD MATCHA AS WELL TO ADD A BIT OF MORE WEIGHT LOSS AGENT.

GET A QUICK SHAKE IN THE MORNING!

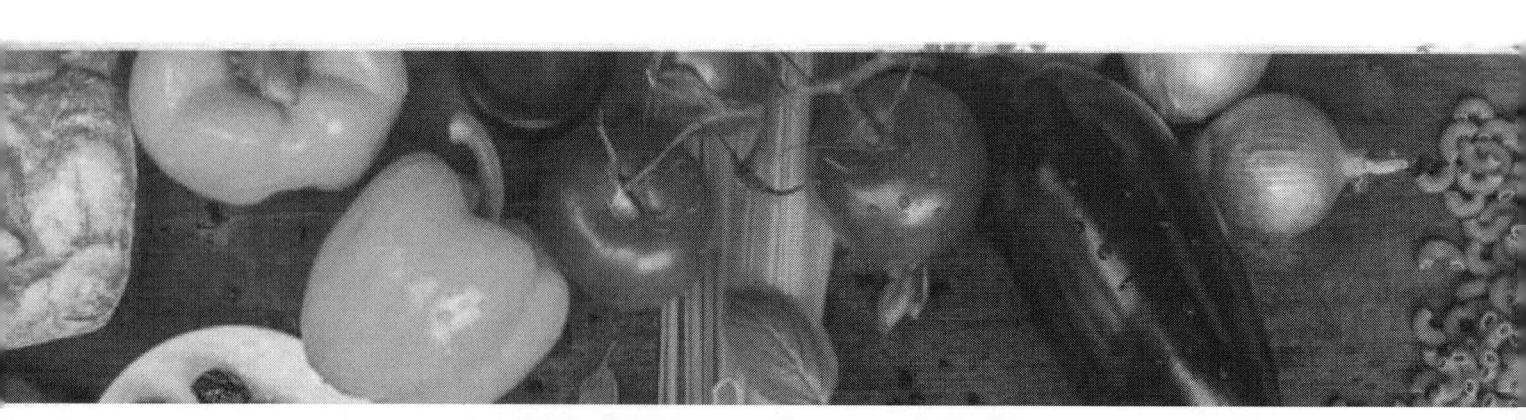

VANILLA WAFFLES

SERVING: 4 PERSONS
COOKING TIME: 15 MIN

CARBS: 70G
PROTEIN: 68G
FATS: 112G
FIBER: 16G
SODIUM: 1421MG
CALORIES: 1532KCAL

INGREDIENTS

- 1 CUP SHREDDED MOZZARELLA CHEESE
- ½ CUP ALMOND FLOUR
- ½ CUP COCONUT FLOUR
- FEW DROPS OF VANILLA ESSENCE
- 1 TSP MONK FRUIT BLEND
- 2 EGGS
- 1 TSP BAKING POWDER
- ¼ CUP CREAM
- 2 TBSP PEANUT BUTTER
- 2 TBSP ROUGHLY CHOPPED HAZELNUTS

INSTRUCTIONS

- COMBINE THE DRY INGREDIENTS IN A BOWL.
- ADD IN VANILLA ESSENCE. THEN ADD EGGS AND MIX THEM WELL.
- MAKE THE WAFFLES IN JUST 2-4 MINUTES.
- COMBINE THE PEANUT BUTTER WITH HAZELNUTS IN A BOWL. FOLD IN CREAM AND DRIZZLE ALL OVER THE WAFFLE.

TARRAGON FRITTATA

SERVING: 2 PERSONS
COOKING TIME: 20 MIN

CARBS: 20G
PROTEIN: 30G
FATS: 49G
FIBER: 7.3G
SODIUM: 714MG
CALORIES: 620 KCAL

INGREDIENTS

- 1 TBSP AVOCADO OIL
- 200G MUSHROOMS
- 2 PORK SAUSAGE
- 1 GARLIC CLOVE
- 100G ASPARAGUS
- 2 LARGE EGGS
- 2 TBSP CREAM
- 1 TBSP WHOLEGRAIN MUSTARD
- 1 TBSP TARRAGON

INSTRUCTIONS

- HEAT THE GRILL AND AVOCADO OIL IN A NON-STICK FRYING PAN THEN ADD MUSHROOMS AND FRY FOR 3 MINUTES.
- SQUEEZE THE SAUSAGE MEAT OUT OF THE SKIN AND TURN INTO NUGGETS AND ADD IN THE FRYING PAN FOR 5 MINUTES UNTIL IT GETS BROWN.
- ADD GARLIC AND ASPARAGUS TOGETHER AND IT COOKS FOR 1 MINUTE.
- WHISK EGGS, CREAM, MUSTARD, TARRAGON IN A SEPARATE BOWL AND SEASON IT WELL.
- POUR EGG INTO THE PAN AND COOL FOR 2-5 MINUTES. GRILL IT FOR 2-3 MINUTES UNTIL IT IS COOKED PROPERLY.
- SERVE WITH GREEN SALAD LEAVES IN THE MIDDLE.

COCONUT CHEESECAKE

SERVING: 2 PERSONS
COOKING TIME: 15 MIN

CARBS: 106G
PROTEIN: 51G
FATS: 107G
FIBER: 13G
SODIUM: 954MG
CALORIES: 1624KCAL

INGREDIENTS

- ½ CUP COCONUT FLOUR
- 2 TBSP ZERO CARBS ARTIFICIAL SWEETENER
- ¼ CUP PEANUT BUTTER
- ½ CUP RICOTTA CHEESE
- ¼ CUP COCONUT CREAM
- ¼ CUP CREAM CHEESE
- ¼ CUP OF COCONUT CUBES
- ¼ CUP CRUSHED CASHEW NUTS

INSTRUCTIONS

- MELT THE PEANUT BUTTER IN THE MICROWAVE FOR 30 SECONDS.
- ADD IN COCONUT FLOUR AND HALF OF THE ARTIFICIAL SWEETENER IN IT.
- MAKE A THICK GRAINY BATTER AND ALIGN IT IN THE DISH. LET IT COOL DOWN FOR 1-2 HOURS.
- BEAT THE CREAM CHEESE, RICOTTA CHEESE IN A BOWL.
- ADD IN COCONUT CREAM AND LEFTOVER ARTIFICIAL SWEETENER AND BEAT IT WELL FOR AROUND 2-3 MINUTES.
- PUT IN COCONUT CUBES AND CRUSHED NUTS AND FOLD THEM.
- LAYER ON THE CHILLED FLOUR LAYER AND LET IT COOL DOWN FOR 4-5 HOURS.

SETTLE YOUR CRAVING WITH CHILLED LOW CARB DESSERT!

INSTANT WRAPS

SERVING: 1 PERSONS
COOKING TIME: 10-15 MIN

CARBS: 2.8G
PROTEIN: 6.9G
FATS: 18G
FIBER: 0.7G
SODIUM: 328MG
CALORIES: 202 KCAL

INGREDIENTS

- 1 LARGE EGG
- 1 TBSP OLIVE OIL
- 2 TBSP TOMATO SALSA
- 1 TBSP FRESH CORIANDER

INSTRUCTIONS

- BEAT THE EGG AND THEN ADD 1 TBSP WATER. HEAT THE OLIVE OIL IN A MEDIUM NON-STICK PAN.
- SPREAD EGG ON THE BASE OF THE PAN, LIKE YOU ARE MAKING PANCAKES. COOK IT UNTIL IT IS SET.
- DON'T TURN THE SIDES LET IT COOK. PLACE THE EGG PANCAKE INTO A PLATTER AND THEN SPREAD TOMATO SALSA AND CORIANDER. ROLL THE EGG AND EAT WHEN IT GETS A BIT COOL.

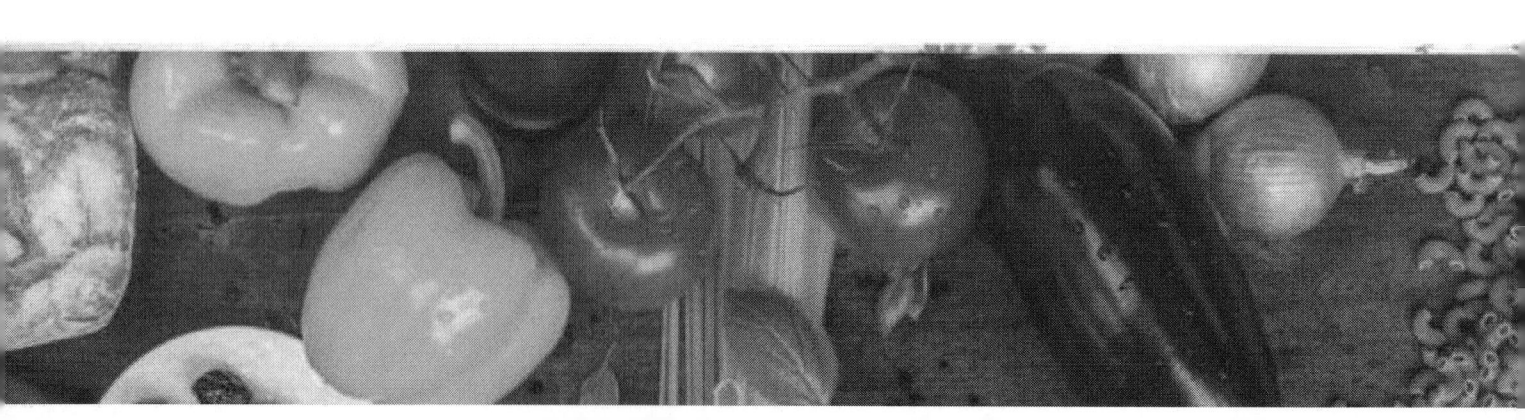

CORDON BLEU CHICKEN

SERVING: 2 PERSONS
COOKING TIME: 15 MIN

CARBS: 37G
PROTEIN: 199G
FATS: 122G
FIBER: 19G
SODIUM: 1826MG
CALORIES: 2025KCAL

INGREDIENTS

- 1 LB CHICKEN BREAST
- 1 CUP SHREDDED CHEESE
- ½ CUP OLIVES
- ½ CUP CHOPPED CHIVES
- 1 TSP THYME
- ½ TSP OREGANO
- SALT TO TASTE
- PEPPER TO TASTE
- 1 EGG
- 1 CUP ALMOND FLOUR
- 1 TSP PAPRIKA

INSTRUCTIONS

- CUT THE CHICKEN BREAST INTO FILLETS.
- CUT FROM THE CENTER OF THE FILLETS AND CREATE A POCKET.
- COMBINE THE CHEESE WITH ALL THE SEASONINGS IN A BOWL. DUMP IN OLIVES AND CHIVES TOO.
- STUFF IN THE CHICKEN POCKET AND DIP IN THE EGG.
- MIX PAPRIKA IN THE ALMOND FLOUR. THEN FOLD FILLETS IN THE ALMOND FLOUR.
- BAKE IT AT 375°F FOR 25 MINUTES. HAVE A DELICIOUS CHEESY CHICKEN!

GREENERY EGG

SERVING: 2 PERSONS
COOKING TIME: 15-20 MIN

CARBS: 32G
PROTEIN: 24G
FATS: 25G
FIBER: 8.4G
SODIUM: 1482MG
CALORIES: 425 KCAL

INGREDIENTS

- ½ TSP GRAPESEED OIL
- ½ TSP SALT
- 200G SPINACH
- 2 LEEKS (SLICED)
- ½ TSP BLACK PEPPER
- 2 GARLIC CLOVES
- ½ TSP CORIANDER SEEDS
- ½ TSP CHILI FLAKES
- 2 LARGE EGGS
- 2 TBSP GREEK YOGURT

INSTRUCTIONS

- HEAT THE FRYING PAN WITH THE GRAPESEED OIL. ADD LEEKS, SALT, AND COOK UNTIL IT GETS SOFT. ADD THE GARLIC, CORIANDER, AND CHILI FLAKES.
- WHEN THE SEEDS BEGIN TO BREAK ADD-IN SPINACH AND LET IT HEAT. POUR OIL INTO THE PAN, THEN CRACK EGGS AND LET IT COOK WHEN IT ATTAINS ITS BROWN COLOR.
- STIR THE YOGURT OVER THE SPINACH AND MIX IT WITH SEASONING.
- TAKE A PLATE, ADD-IN IN SPINACH MIXTURE AND FRY AN EGG AND SPRINKLE BLACK PEPPER, LEMON, AND CHILI FLAKES TO HAVE A HEALTHY BREAKFAST!

BAKED VEGGIES

SERVING: 2 PERSONS
COOKING TIME: 20 MIN

CARBS: 52G
PROTEIN: 62G
FATS: 68G
FIBER: 20G
SODIUM: 1835MG
CALORIES: 1105KCAL

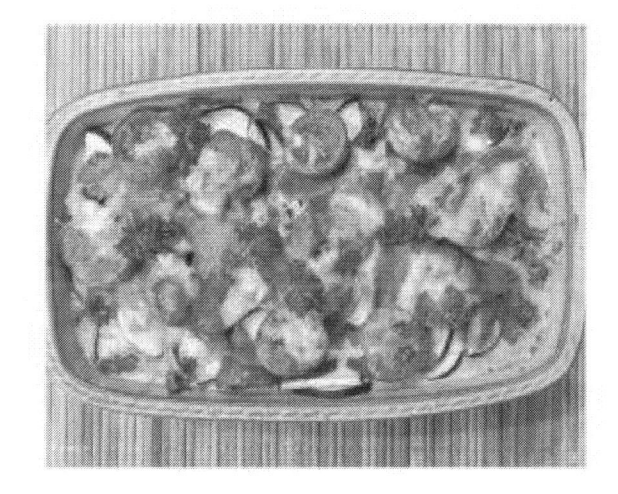

INGREDIENTS

- ½ ZUCCHINI
- 1 TOMATO
- 1 EGGPLANT
- ½ CUP BROCCOLI FLORETS
- SALT TO TASTE
- PEPPER TO TASTE
- 1 TBSP LEMON JUICE
- 1 CUP MOZZARELLA CHEESE
- 1 CUP CHEDDAR CHEESE
- ½ TSP THYME
- ½ TSP OREGANO

INSTRUCTIONS

- CUT THE 1 INCH THICK ROUND SLICES OF ZUCCHINI, TOMATO, AND EGGPLANT.
- BLANCH THE BROCCOLI FLORETS, ZUCCHINI, AND EGGPLANT FOR 3-4 MINUTES.
- SEASON THE VEGGIES WITH SALT, PEPPER, AND LEMON JUICE.
- ALIGN THEM IN THE BAKING TRAY AND SPRINKLE THE WHOLE CHEESE ON THE TOP.
- SPRINKLE THYME AND OREGANO ON THE CHEESE.
- POP IN THE OVEN AT 375°F FOR 15 MINUTES. HERE COME THE SIZZLING CHEESY VEGGIES

BAKED TOMATO EGGS

SERVING: 4 PERSONS
COOKING TIME: 30 MIN

CARBS: 24G
PROTEIN: 30G
FATS: 61G
FIBER: 6.3G
SODIUM: 315MG
CALORIES: 749 KCAL

INGREDIENTS

- 4 TOMATOES
- 3 CLOVE GARLIC
- 3 TBSP OLIVE OIL
- 4 EGGS
- 2 TBSP PARSLEY

INSTRUCTIONS

- PREHEAT THE OVEN TO 200 DEGREES. CUT THE TOMATOES INTO SMALL WEDGES AND SPREAD THEM IN AN OVEN DISH.
- PEEL THE GARLIC AND SLICE IT THIN. SPREAD THIN SLICES OF GARLIC OVER THE DISH AND THEN ADD TOMATOES.
- DRIZZLE OLIVE OIL, SALT, PEPPER, AND STIR ALL THE INGREDIENTS TOGETHER UNTIL TOMATOES BECOME GLIST.
- PUT THE DISH INTO THE OVEN AND BAKE IT FOR 25 MINUTES UNTIL TOMATOES BECOME SOFT.
- MAKE GAPS BETWEEN TOMATOES, BREAK AN EGG, AND PUT EGGS IN DIFFERENT GAPS.
- PUT IN THE OVEN AND COOK FOR 5-10 MINUTES UNTIL THE EGGS ARE COOKED. SCATTER WITH FRESH PARSLEY AND YOU ARE READY TO GO!

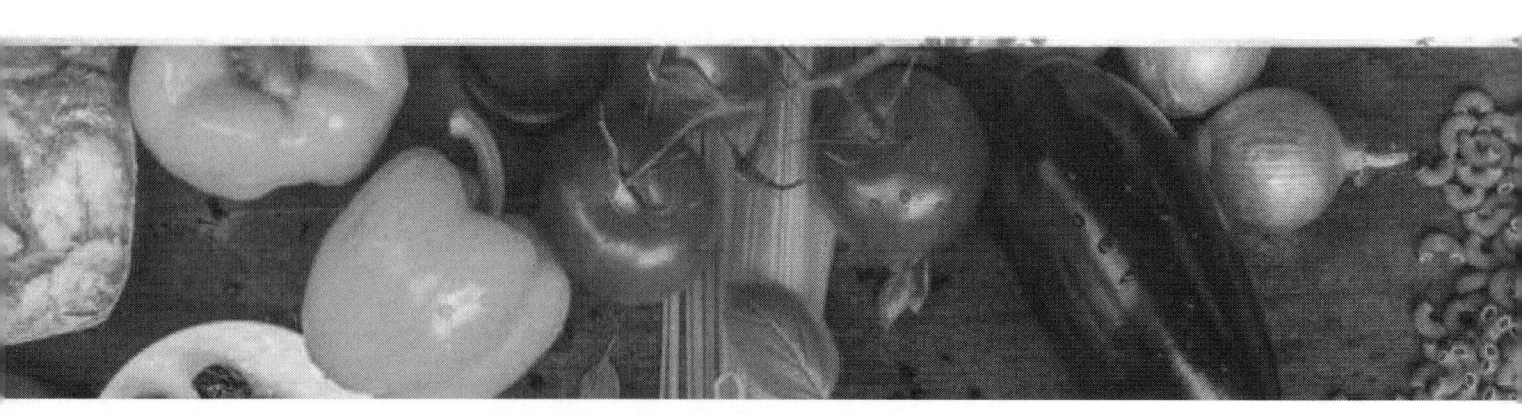

CHEESE HASH BROWNS

SERVING: 2 PERSONS
COOKING TIME: 15 MIN

CARBS: 15G
PROTEIN: 30G
FATS: 28G
FIBER: 2.7G
SODIUM: 1325MG
CALORIES: 425KCAL

INGREDIENTS

- ½ CUP MOZZARELLA CHEESE SPRINKLES
- ½ CUP PARMESAN CHEESE
- ½ CUP FINELY CHOPPED SPINACH
- 4 TBSP FINELY CHOPPED PARSLEY

INSTRUCTIONS

- MIX UP THE SPINACH AND PARSLEY IN A BOWL.
- ADD IN PARMESAN CHEESE AND MOZZARELLA CHEESE SPRINKLES. MIX IT NICELY.
- TAKE A MUFFIN TRAY AND GIVE IT AN OLIVE OIL SPRAY.
- SPREAD THE MIXTURE AT THE BASE AND MAKE A THIN LAYER OF IT.
- BAKE IT AT 375°F FOR 10-12 MINUTES.

EGG FAJITA

SERVING: 2 PERSONS
COOKING TIME: 20 MIN

CARBS: 39G
PROTEIN: 94G
FATS: 101G
FIBER: 6.6G
SODIUM: 1293MG
CALORIES: 1441KCAL

INGREDIENTS

- 4 EGGS
- ½ CUP MILK
- SALT TO TASTE
- PEPPER TO TASTE
- 1 TSP BASIL LEAVES
- 1 RED BELL PEPPER
- 1 YELLOW BELL PEPPER
- ¼ CUP MUSHROOMS
- ½ LB PORK MINCE
- 1 TSP SESAME SEEDS
- 2 TBSP AVOCADO OIL
- 1 TSP GARLIC PASTE
- ½ TSP GARAM MASALA
- 2 TBSP TOMATO PASTE

INSTRUCTIONS

- HEAT THE OIL IN THE PAN. SAUTE GARLIC PASTE IN IT.
- DUMP IN PORK MINCE AND COOK FOR 4-5 MINUTES UNTIL IT CHANGES ITS COLOR.
- ADD IN TOMATO PASTE, SALT AND LET IT COOK FOR 2 MINUTES. AND ADD GARAM MASALA IN IT.
- NOW ADD BELL PEPPER STRIPS TO IT. SAUTE A BIT
- NOW CRACK EGGS IN THE PAN. SEASON IT WITH SALT, PEPPER, AND BASIL LEAVES.
- ADD MUSHROOMS TO IT AND COOK FOR 4-5 MINUTES WITH THE LID ON THE PAN.
- SPRINKLE SESAME SEEDS IN THE END.

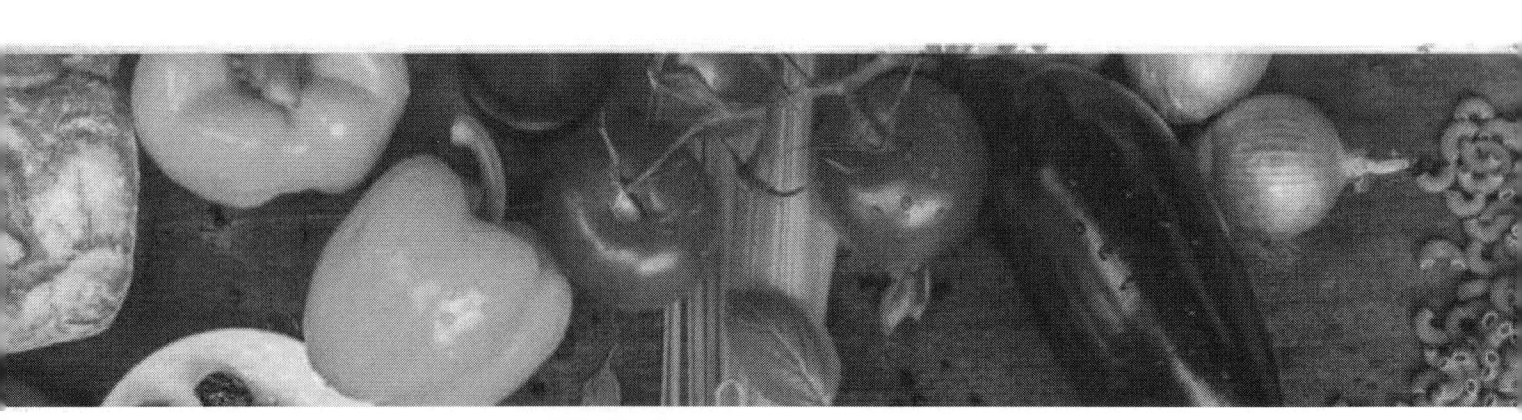

LAMB AND BROCCOLI

SERVING: 2 PERSONS
COOKING TIME: 15 MIN

CARBS: 59G
PROTEIN: 119G
FATS: 96G
FIBER: 19G
SODIUM: 1876MG
CALORIES: 1563 KCAL

INGREDIENTS

- 25G BUTTER
- 4 LAMB NECK FILLETS (CUT IN CHUNKS)
- ½ CUP SCAPERS
- ½ TSP SALT
- ½ TSP BLACK PEPPER
- 150ML CHICKEN STOCK
- 1 CUP BROCCOLI

INSTRUCTIONS

- HEAT THE FRYING PAN WITH BUTTER UNTIL IT STARTS SIZZLING, THEN ADD THE LAMB.
- SEASON WITH SALT, BLACK PEPPER, AND COOK IT FOR 7-8 MINUTES WHEN ITS SIDES BECOME BROWN.
- SCATTER SCAPERS AND POUR IN THE STOCK, THEN SIMMER IT GENTLY AND COOK UNTIL SCAPERS BECOME DEFORESTED.
- ADD BROCCOLI TO A PAN AND SIMMER FOR 1-2 MINUTES. MAKE SURE IT IS A VIBRANT GREEN. SERVE TASTY FOOD WITH FRIENDS!

ROASTED PLATTER

SERVING: 2 PERSONS
COOKING TIME: 15-20 MIN

CARBS: 45G
PROTEIN: 34G
FATS: 39G
FIBER: 8.6G
SODIUM: 697MG
CALORIES: 668 KCAL

INGREDIENTS

- 1 TBSP COCONUT OIL
- ½ ASPARAGUS (CUT INTO 5CM PIECES)
- 100G PEAS
- 50G FETA CHEESE
- 1 TBSP CHOPPED MINT
- 3 LARGE EGGS
- 1 TBSP BALSAMIC VINEGAR
- 2 TOMATOES

INSTRUCTIONS

- HEAT THE OVEN TO 180C. PUT THE COCONUT OIL IN THE SMALL DISH. PLACE IN THE OVEN FOR 2-3 MINUTES THEN ADD ASPARAGUS AND PEAS INTO HOT OIL AND GENTLY TOSS IT.
- REMOVE THE PAN FROM THE OVEN AND CRUMBLE WITH FETA OVER IT. MEANWHILE, BEAT THE EGGS AND SEASON WITH GROUND BLACK PEPPER.
- REMOVE THE DISH FROM THE OVEN AND POUR EGGS OVER IT AND THEN BAKE IT FOR 15 MINUTES UNTIL EGGS ARE COOKED.
- CUT THE TOMATOES AND ROAST IT.
- DRIZZLE BALSAMIC VINEGAR OVER ROAST TOMATOES. SERVE DELICIOUS, WITH ROASTED AND CRISPY SALAD.

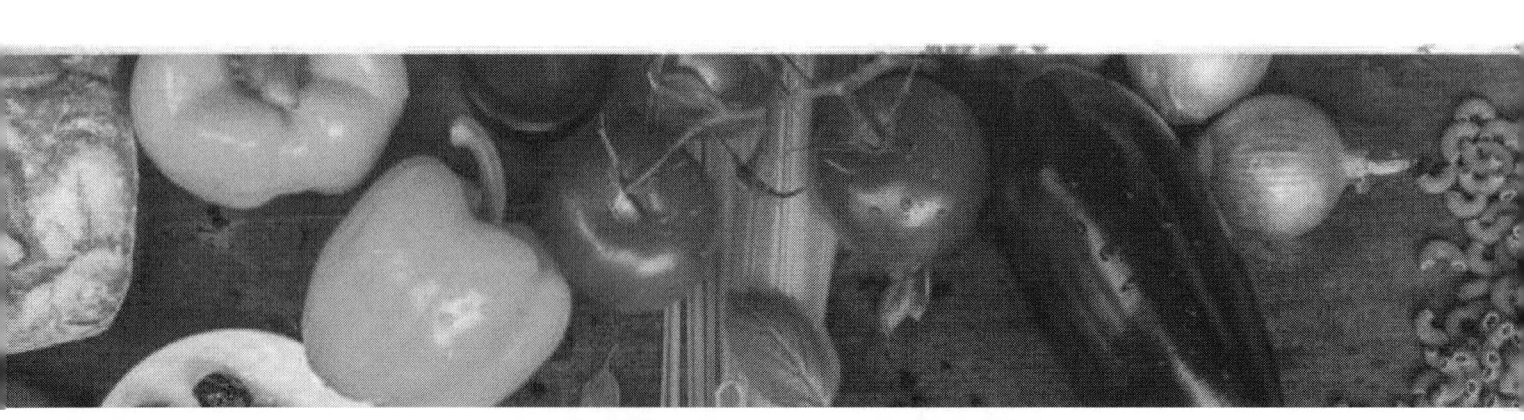

ROASTED LAMB FILLETS

SERVING: 2 PERSONS
COOKING TIME: 15 MIN

CARBS: 26G
PROTEIN: 108G
FATS: 95G
FIBER: 7.6G
SODIUM: 1858MG
CALORIES: 1385 KCAL

INGREDIENTS

- 25G BUTTER
- 4 LAMB NECK FILLETS
- ½ TSP SALT
- ½ BLACK PEPPER
- 2 HANDFUL OF PEAS
- 150ML CHICKEN STOCK
- 3 LETTUCE LEAVES (CUT INTO QUARTERS)

INSTRUCTIONS

- HEAT THE BUTTER IN THE NON-STICK PAN UNTIL IT GETS SIZZLING. ADD LAMB AND SEASON WITH SALT AND BLACK PEPPER.
- COOK FOR 6-7 MINUTES UNTIL ALL THE EDGES BECOME BROWN.
- SCATTER PEAS AND POUR IN THE STOCK AND LET IT SIMMER UNTIL DEFROSTED.
- ADD LETTUCE TO THE PAN AND SIMMER FOR 5-10 MINUTES UNTIL IT'S STILL VIBRANT GREEN. HAVE A TASTY DAY!

BEEF PARSLEY MIX

SERVING: 2 PERSONS
COOKING TIME: 10-15 MIN

CARBS: 18G
PROTEIN: 27G
FATS: 99G
FIBER: 5.5G
SODIUM: 548MG
CALORIES: 1049 KCAL

INGREDIENTS

- 2 SALAD LEAVES
- 175G TOMATOES (HALVES)
- 4-5 ROASTED PEPPER
- 8-12 SLICES OF ROASTED BEEF FOR DRESSING
- 2 TBSP LEMON JUICE
- 1 TBSP MUSTARD
- 3 TBSP PARSLEY (CHOPPED)
- 5 TBSP OLIVE OIL

INSTRUCTIONS

- SCATTER THE SALAD LEAVES, TOMATOES, AND RED PEPPER OVER THE PLATTER, ARRANGE THE SLICES OF BEEF ON THE TOP OF IT.
- PUT LEMON JUICE, MUSTARD, PARSLEY INTO A SMALL BOWL AND ADD SOME SALT AND PEPPER, WHISK IT WELL UNTIL IT BECOMES THICK.
- DRIZZLE OVER THE COOKED BEEF AND SALAD. NOW IT IS READY TO EAT!

AVOCADO AND PRAWN COCKTAIL

SERVING: 1 PERSONS
COOKING TIME: 15 MIN

CARBS: 64G
PROTEIN: 53G
FATS: 88G
FIBER: 20G
SODIUM: 3115MG
CALORIES: 1213 KCAL

INGREDIENTS

FOR DRESSING
- 4 TBSP OLIVE OIL
- 1 LEMON JUICED
- ½ TSP SALT
- ½ TSP CAYENNE PEPPER

FOR SALAD
- 1 AVOCADO
- 200G COOKED PRAWN
- 3 SPRING ONIONS

FOR TOPPING
- 2 TBSP CORIANDER
- 2 TBSP CREAM CHEESE

INSTRUCTIONS

- FIRST OF ALL, MAKE A DRESSING BY MIXING OLIVE OIL, CITRUS JUICE IN A SEPARATE BOWL AND ADD SALT AND CAYENNE PEPPER.
- TAKE A BOWL AND ADD SLICED AVOCADO, COOKED PRAWN, AND ONION SPRINGS AND MIX IT WITH DRESSING.
- TAKE MARTINI GLASSES AND POUR THE AVOCADO COCKTAIL IN THE CENTER.
- DRIZZLE REMAINING DRESSING AND THEN TOP WITH CORIANDER AND CREAM CHEESE BEFORE SERVING!

PIGEON MEAL

SERVING: 2 PERSONS
COOKING TIME: 10 MIN

CARBS: 70G
PROTEIN: 20G
FATS: 131G
FIBER: 19G
SODIUM: 2759MG
CALORIES: 1467 KCAL

INGREDIENTS

- 1 TBSP OLIVE OIL
- 1 CLOVE GARLIC
- 1 ROSEMARY
- ½ TSP PAPRIKA
- ½ TSP SALT
- 1 TBSP VINEGAR
- 4 PIGEON BREAST
- 1 CUP DRIED TOMATOES
- 100G TOASTED HAZELNUT

FOR DRESSING
- 1 TBSP BALSAMIC VINEGAR
- 3 TBSP OLIVE OIL
- ½ TSP SALT
- ½ TSP BLACK PEPPER

INSTRUCTIONS

- MAKE THE SAUCE WITH SALT, PEPPER, BALSAMIC VINEGAR, AND OLIVE OIL.
- HEAT THE OIL IN THE FRYING PAN, THEN ADD GARLIC, ROSEMARY, SALT, PAPRIKA, VINEGAR, AND SEASON PIGEON BREAST. COOK FOR 3-4 MINUTES.
- ARRANGE THE TOMATOES IN THE BOWL. ALSO, SLICE THE PIGEON BREAST WHEN IT IS COOKED PROPERLY.
- SCATTER HAZELNUT AND DRIZZLE SEASONING FOR AN OUTSTANDING TASTE!

PRAWN COCONUT CURRY

SERVING: 2 PERSONS
COOKING TIME: 10 MIN

CARBS: 240G
PROTEIN: 131G
FATS: 110G
FIBER: 15G
SODIUM: 7139MG
CALORIES: 2432 KCAL

INGREDIENTS

- 2 TBSP OLIVE OIL
- 1 ONION (THIN SLICED)
- 2 TBSP TOMATO PUREE
- 2 CLOVE GARLIC
- 1 GREEN CHILI
- 3 TBSP CURRY PASTE
- 200ML VEGETABLE STOCK
- 200ML COCONUT CREAM
- 350G RAW PRAWNS

FOR TOPPING

- ¼ CUP CORIANDER
- ¼ CUP CRUSHED ALMONDS

INSTRUCTIONS

- HEAT THE OIL IN THE FRYING PAN, THEN ADD THIN SLICES OF ONIONS, GARLIC, AND HALF CHILI, COOK FOR 5-6 MINUTES UNTIL IT BECOMES SOFT.
- ADD CURRY PASTE AND COOK FOR MORE THAN 1-2 MINUTES.
- ADD TOMATO PUREE, STOCK, AND COCONUT CREAM. SIMMER ALL THE INGREDIENTS FOR 10 MINUTES, THEN ADD PRAWNS. COOK FOR 3 MIN UNTIL THEY TURN OPAQUE.
- TOP WITH CORIANDER AND CRUSHED ALMOND NUTS.
- SCATTER GREEN CHILIES, THEN SERVE WITH CAULIFLOWER RICE!

HERB ZUCCHINI OMELET

SERVING: PERSONS
COOKING TIME: 10-15 MIN

CARBS: 30G
PROTEIN: 13G
FATS: 8.6G
FIBER: 11G
SODIUM: 1198MG
CALORIES: 207 KCAL

INGREDIENTS

- 1 TSP GRAPESEED OIL
- 1 ZUCCHINI
- ½ TSP SALT
- ½ TSP CAYENNE PEPPER
- 2 EGGS
- 1 TBSP CHOPPED PARSLEY
- 1 TBSP CHOPPED BASIL
- ½ CUP SHREDDED CHEESE

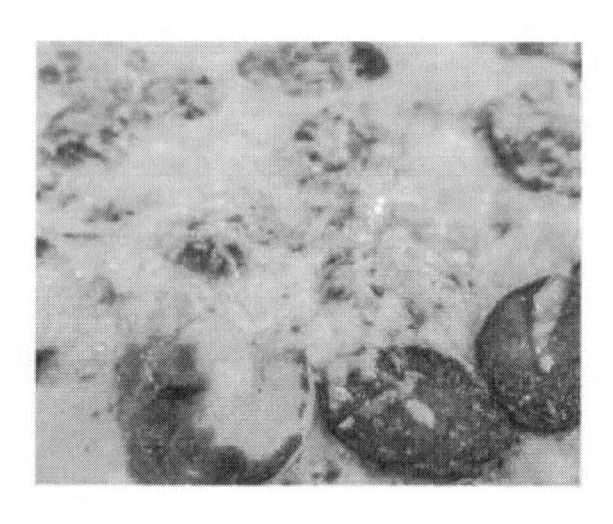

INSTRUCTIONS

- CUT THE ZUCCHINI INTO AROUND SHAPE SLICES, THEN HEAT THE NON-STICK PAN WITH RAPESEED OIL.
- COOK ZUCCHINI FOR 5-6 MINUTES UNTIL IT BECOMES SOFT AND ATTAINS ITS BROWN COLOR.
- BEAT THE EGGS BY ADDING HERBS AND THEN ADD CAYENNE PEPPER IN A SEPARATE SMALL BOWL.
- TAKE OUT ZUCCHINI FROM THE PAN AND PUT THEM ON SERVING PLATES.
- POUR EGG MIXTURE INTO THE PAN AND DON'T STIR UNTIL THE BASE IS SET.
- ALLOW TO SET THE OMELET AND LET IT COOK PROPERLY. CUT INTO QUARTERS AND LAYER THE FRIED ZUCCHINI.
- TOP UP WITH CHEESE AND HAVE A CHEESY VEGGIE OMELET.

SHRIMPS WITH VEGGIES

SERVING: 2 PERSONS
COOKING TIME: 25 MIN

CARBS: 209G
PROTEIN: 109G
FATS: 39G
FIBER: 18G
SODIUM: 6412MG
CALORIES: 1613 KCAL

INGREDIENTS

- 2 LIMES
- 1 RED BELL PEPPER
- ½ GREEN BELL PEPPER
- ½ YELLOW ONION (THIN-SLICED)
- 2 TSP CANOLA OIL
- 2 GARLIC CLOVES
- 1 TSP KOSHER SALT
- ½ TSP OREGANO
- ½ TSP CHILI POWDER
- ½ TSP PAPRIKA
- ½ TSP CAYENNE PEPPER
- ¼ TSP GROUND CUMIN
- 1 LB RAW SHRIMP
- SOUR CREAM/ GREEK YOGURT

INSTRUCTIONS

- POUR LIME JUICE AND GARLIC IN A BLENDER, THEN ADD OIL, SALT, AND SPICES AND COMBINE IT WELL.
- MARINATE THE SHRIMPS WITH THIS BLEND AND LEAVE IT FOR 15 MINUTES.
- ROAST SHRIMPS ONTO THE PAN. ADD THE BELL PEPPERS AND ROAST IT FOR ABOUT 8 MINUTES.

PUMPKIN SPAGHETTI

SERVING: 2 PERSONS
COOKING TIME: 15 MIN

CARBS: 24G
PROTEIN: 44G
FATS: 84G
FIBER: 7.9G
SODIUM: 3672MG
CALORIES: 1000 KCAL

INGREDIENTS

- 1 BUTTERNUT PUMPKIN
- 1 SAGE LEAVES
- 2 CLOVE GARLIC (CHOPPED)
- 4 SLICES PROSCIUTTO
- ⅓ CUP ALMONDS (CHOPPED)
- 60G BUTTER

INSTRUCTIONS

- PREHEAT THE OVEN TO 250°C. USE A VEGETABLE PEELER, THEN TURN THE PUMPKIN INTO SPAGHETTI.
- SPREAD OVER THE BAKING PAN AND TOP UP WITH SAGE LEAVES, CHOPPED GARLIC, PROSCIUTTO, AND CHOPPED ALMONDS. SCATTER BUTTER OVER THE TRAY FOR THE PERFECT TASTE.
- BAKE FOR ABOUT 10-12 MINUTES. MAKE SURE IT'S COLOR BECOMES NUTTY BROWN AND THE PROSCIUTTO IS CRISPY.
- TOSS THE PUMPKIN TO COAT WITH BUTTER. SERVE WITH CRUSHED ALMONDS NUTS.

BHAJI BURGER

SERVING: 3 PERSONS
COOKING TIME: 20 MIN

CARBS: 132G
PROTEIN: 148G
FATS: 195G
FIBER: 21G
SODIUM: 2283MG
CALORIES: 2846KCAL

INGREDIENTS

FOR PATTIES
- 400G LAMB (MINCE)
- 2 TBSP TANDOORI PASTE
- ½ TSP SALT
- 1 TSP CUMIN SEEDS

FOR SAUCE
- ½ CUCUMBER
- 150G PLAIN YOGURT
- 2 TBSP SMALL MINT LEAVES

FOR BHAJIS
- 100G ALMOND FLOUR
- 1 TBSP GARAM MASALA
- 1 TSP BAKING SODA
- 1 CHOPPED ONION
- 3 TBSP SUNFLOWER OIL

INSTRUCTIONS

- PUT MINCED LAMB AND ALL THE SEASONINGS INTO A SMALL BOWL, THEN ADD SALT AND SQUEEZE IT WITH YOUR FINGERS. SHAPE INTO THREE PATTIES AND OUT IN THE FRIDGE.
- GRATE THE CUCUMBER AND PUT IT IN PLAIN YOGURT.
- ADD MINT, AND A PINCH OF SALT. MIX IT AND CHILL.
- FOR BHAJIS, TIP THE ALMOND FLOUR, SPICES, SALT, AND SODA IN A BOWL. GRADUALLY ADD 200ML COLD WATER TO MAKE A THICK BATTER, THEN MIX ONION IN IT. CHOP ONION BEFORE MIXING.
- HEAT THE SUNFLOWER OIL IN A FRYING PAN AND THEN ADD BETTER TO HAVE THREE BURGER SIZE BHAJIS. COOK FOR 3 MINUTES UNTIL ONE SIDE GETS CRISPY. FLIP THE SIDE AND COOK FOR ANOTHER 2-3 MINUTES.
- PUT LETTUCE, PATTIE, RAITA, RED ONION, AND FOLD THE BHAJI.

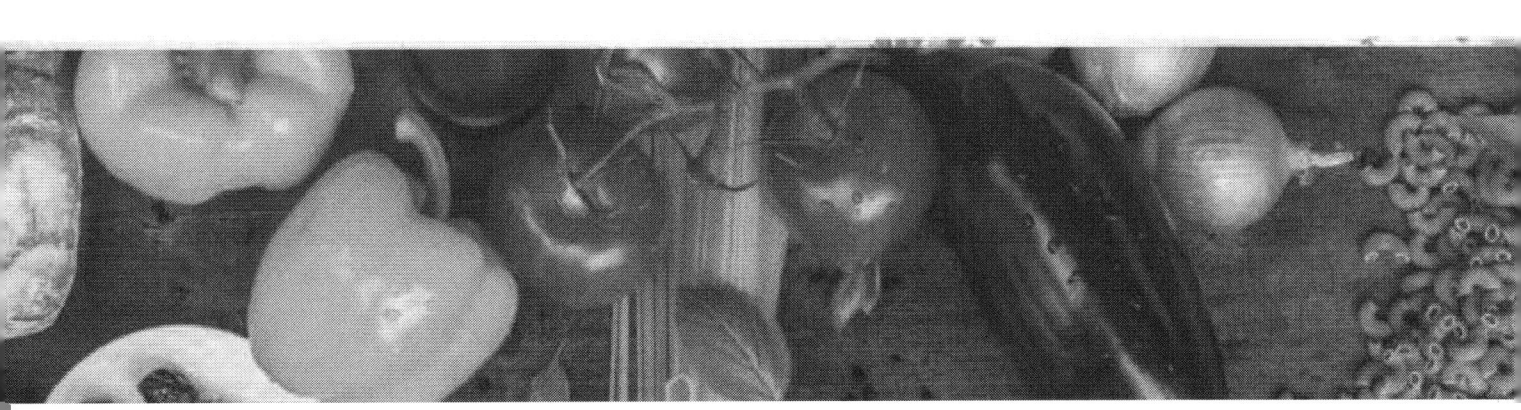

PANCAKES

SERVING: 2 PERSONS
COOKING TIME: 25 MIN

CARBS: 40G
PROTEIN: 42G
FATS: 84G
FIBER: 16G
SODIUM: 298MG
CALORIES: 1029 KCAL

INGREDIENTS

- 125G ALMOND FLOUR
- 1 EGG
- 250ML MILK
- 100G BUTTER

INSTRUCTIONS

- PUT ALMOND FLOUR IN A BOWL AND WHISK THE EGG IN IT.
- NOW ADD MILK TO IT AND WHISK IT AGAIN.
- LEAVE IT FOR 20 MINUTES.
- WHEN YOU USE IT TO MAKE SURE YOU STIR IT AGAIN.
- HEAT NON-STICK FRYING PAN WITH BUTTER.
- ADD A SINGLE SERVING SPOON OF BATTER INTO THE PAN AND COOK IT FOR A FEW MINS UNTIL THE LAYER BECOMES GOLDEN BROWN.
- FLIP THE SIDE AND COOK FOR ANOTHER 2-3 MINUTES. REPEAT UNTIL ALL THE MIXTURE HAS BEEN CONSUMED.
- SERVE WITH PEANUT BUTTER TO HAVE A YUMMY TASTE!

KINGFISH LETTUCE WRAPS

SERVING: 4 PERSONS
COOKING TIME: 10-15 MIN

CARBS: 59G
PROTEIN: 199G
FATS: 35G
FIBER: 8G
SODIUM: 1975MG
CALORIES: 1371 KCAL

INGREDIENTS

- 800G KIND FISH FILLET
- 2 TBSP PEANUT OIL
- 2 CHOPPED ONIONS
- 4 GARLIC CLOVES (CRUSHED)
- 2 TBSP SOY SAUCE
- 2 TSP FISH SAUCE
- 6-8 LETTUCE LEAVES

INSTRUCTIONS

- PLACE THE KINGFISH IN A FOOD PROCESSOR UNTIL IT IS FULLY CHOPPED.
- HEAT THE FRYING PAN WITH PEANUT OIL, THEN ADD ONION, GARLIC AND COOK FOR 2-3 MINUTES UNTIL IT BECOMES SOFT.
- ADD FISH AND COOK FOR 2 MINUTES, TOSS THE FISH AND COOK FOR ANOTHER 2-4 MINUTES UNTIL IT TURNS INTO A BROWN COLOR.
- ADD SOY SAUCE, FISH SAUCE, AND STIR IT FOR 2-3 MINUTES UNTIL THE SAUCE IS ABSORBED. SERVE WITH LETTUCE LEAVE OVER THE WRAPS!

BROCCOLI MAC & CHEESE

SERVING: 2 PERSONS
COOKING TIME: 20 MIN

CARBS: 34G
PROTEIN: 44G
FATS: 124G
FIBER: 12G
SODIUM: 1929MG
CALORIES: 1327KCAL

INGREDIENTS

- 2 CUPS BROCCOLI
- 1 MINCED GARLIC CLOVE
- ½ CUP CREAM
- 1 CUP CHEDDAR CHEESE
- 10-12 PEPPERONI
- SALT TO TASTE
- PEPPER TO TASTE
- ½ TSP PAPRIKA
- 2 TBSP OLIVE OIL

INSTRUCTIONS

- BOIL THE BROCCOLI IN BOILING WATER FOR 10-12 MINUTES.
- SAUTE GARLIC IN OLIVE OIL AND ADD IN THE CREAM.
- SEASON IT WITH SALT, PEPPER, AND PAPRIKA.
- TEAR THE PEPPERONI ROUGHLY IN SLICES AND DUMP IN THE CREAM. ADD BROCCOLI ALONG WITH IT.
- THEN ADD THE CHEESE AND COOK UNTIL THE CHEESE MELTS.
- MIX UP THE WHOLE BROCCOLI MIXTURE AND SETTLE YOUR CRAVING WITH A CREAMY TREAT!

KETO THAI SALAD

SERVING: 4 PERSONS
COOKING TIME: 20 MIN

CARBS: 54G
PROTEIN: 122G
FATS: 168G
FIBER: 18G
SODIUM: 3327MG
CALORIES: 2125KCAL

INGREDIENTS

- 1 CUP PEANUTS
- ½ LB TURKEY
- 2 BOILED EGGS
- 1 CUCUMBER
- ½ CUP COARSELY CHOPPED ASPARAGUS
- 4-5 CHERRY TOMATOES
- 1 TBSP PUMPKIN SEEDS
- ¼ CUP COCONUT MILK
- 1 TSP BALSAMIC VINEGAR
- SALT TO TASTE
- PEPPER TO TASTE
- 2 TBSP SOY SAUCE
- 4 TBSP OLIVE OIL

INSTRUCTIONS

- MAKE A PEANUT DRESSING BY BLENDING HALF A CUP OF PEANUTS AND COCONUT MILK IN A BLENDER.
- SEASON IT WITH SALT AND PEPPER.
- MARINATE TURKEY FILLETS WITH SALT, PEPPER, AND SOY SAUCE FROM BOTH SIDES.
- HEAT HALF OF THE OLIVE OIL IN THE PAN. COOK FILLETS FROM BOTH SIDES IN THE PAN FOR ABOUT 10 MINUTES.
- LET IT COOL AND SHRED IT WITH THE HELP OF A FORK.
- DICE THE CUCUMBER AND CUT THE BOILED EGGS INTO QUARTERS. CUT THE TOMATOES INTO HALVES.
- COMBINE CUCUMBER, TOMATOES, ASPARAGUS, TURKEY, AND PUMPKIN SEEDS IN A BOWL.
- ADD THE VINEGAR AND HALF OF THE OLIVE OIL AND TOSS IT WELL. ADD IN THE LEFTOVER PEANUTS.
- POUR IN THE DRESSING AND FOLD IT WELL IN THE DRESSING.
- DRIZZLE THE LEFTOVER DRESSING AND EXPLORE THE THAI FLAVORS!

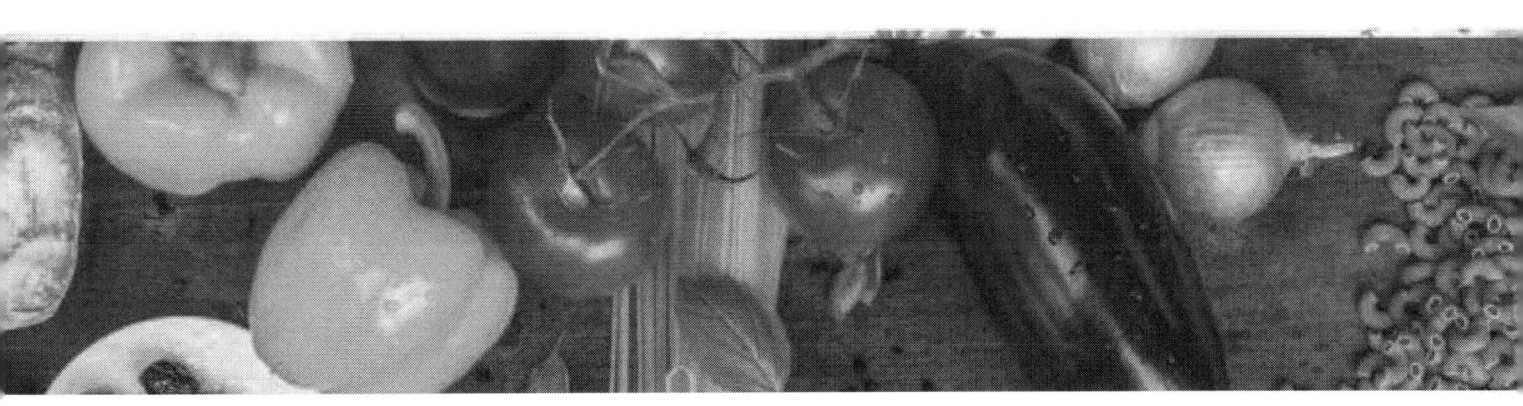

TOMATO ROASTED WINGS

SERVING: 2 PERSONS
COOKING TIME: 30 MIN

CARBS: 59G
PROTEIN: 80G
FATS: 111G
FIBER: 5.8G
SODIUM: 1920MG
CALORIES: 1540KCAL

INGREDIENTS

- 1 LB WINGS
- 2 TOMATOES
- 1 TBSP TOMATO POWDER
- 1 TSP GARLIC POWDER
- SALT TO TASTE
- PEPPER TO TASTE
- 1 TSP LEMON JUICE

INSTRUCTIONS

- MARINATE THE WINGS WITH TOMATO POWDER, GARLIC POWDER, LEMON JUICE, SALT, AND PEPPER.
- CUT THE TOMATOES INTO THICK SPHERICAL SLICES.
- ALIGN THE WINGS IN THE BAKING TRAY AND PLACE THE TOMATO SLICES AMONG THEM.
- BAKE AT 375°F FOR 20 MINUTES AND TAKE OUT THE FLAVORFUL WINGS!

SPINACH FRITTERS WITH SALSA

SERVING: 2 PERSONS
COOKING TIME: 25 MIN

CARBS: 291G
PROTEIN: 115G
FATS: 65G
FIBER: 78G
SODIUM: 1275MG
CALORIES: 2078 KCAL

INGREDIENTS

FOR FRITTERS AND EGGS
- 1 TSP RAPESEED OIL
- 1 RED ONION
- 1 RED PEPPER
- ½ CUP COCONUT FLOUR
- 1 TSP SMOKED PAPRIKA
- 1 TSP CORIANDER
- 1 TSP BAKING POWDER
- 1 CUP CHOPPED SPINACH
- 2 LARGE EGGS

FOR SALSA
- 1 SMALL RED ONION
- 2 DICED TOMATOES
- 1 DICED CUCUMBER
- 30G CORIANDER
- 1 LIME

INSTRUCTIONS

- HEAT THE OVEN TO 200°C AND LINE A LARGE TRAY WITH BAKING PARCHMENT PAPER.
- CHOP ONION, TOMATOES, AND CORIANDER
- HEAT THE RAPESEED OIL IN THE PAN, THEN FRY THE ONION AND PEPPER FOR 5 MINUTES UNTIL IT BECOMES SOFT. MIX COCONUT FLOUR, SPICES, AND BAKING POWDER IN A SEPARATE BOWL. ADD ONIONS, PEPPER, SPINACH, AND GS, AND THEN MIX IT WELL.
- PUT EIGHT MOUNDS IN A BAKING TRAY, IT SHOULD BE WELL-SPACED APART. BAKE FOR 20 MINUTES AND COOK IT UNTIL IT BECOMES GOLDEN.
- MIX SALSA INGREDIENTS BY ADDING ONIONS, TOMATOES, CUCUMBER, LIME, AND CORIANDER.

SAUCY MEATBALLS WITH VEGGIES

SERVING: 4 PERSONS
COOKING TIME: 20 MIN

CARBS: 40G
PROTEIN: 129G
FATS: 144G
FIBER: 7G
SODIUM: 2204MG
CALORIES: 1984KCAL

INGREDIENTS

- 1 LB BEEF
- ¼ CUP CHOPPED SPRING ONION
- 1 CHOPPED ONION
- 2 MINCED GARLIC CLOVES
- ¼ CUP TOMATO PASTE
- 2 TBSP SOY SAUCE
- 1 TBSP WORCESTERSHIRE SAUCE
- ½ CUP CHICKEN BROTH
- ½ RED BELL PEPPER
- ½ GREEN BELL PEPPER
- SALT TO TASTE
- PEPPER TO TASTE
- 4 TBSP OLIVE OIL

INSTRUCTIONS

- COMBINE BEEF, SPRING ONION, WHITE ONION, IN A BOWL.
- SEASON IT WITH SALT AND PEPPER AND MIX IT WELL.
- SHAPE UP 12-15 MEATBALLS OUT OF IT.
- HEAT THE OLIVE OIL IN A PAN AND SAUTE MINCED GARLIC IN IT.
- PUT HALF OF THE MEATBALLS IN IT AND COOK THEM FOR AROUND 2-3 MINUTES.
- PUT IN TOMATO SAUCE, SOY SAUCE, AND WORCESTERSHIRE SAUCE. STIR IT
- SEASON WITH SALT AND PEPPER AND ADD IN CHICKEN BROTH.
- LET IT SIMMER FOR AROUND 2 MIN AND ADD CUBED PEPPERS TO IT. COOK IT FOR 2-3 MINUTES AND THE SAUCY MEAL IS READY TO EAT WITH LOW CARB RICE!

MOROCCAN CHICKEN

SERVING: 4 PERSONS
COOKING TIME: 30 MIN

CARBS: 33G
PROTEIN: 22G
FATS: 36G
FIBER: 5.7G
SODIUM: 4510MG
CALORIES: 514 KCAL

INGREDIENTS

- 3 LB WHOLE CHICKEN
- ¼ CUP RAS EL HANOUT (MOROCCAN SPICE)
- 1 CUP THICK YOGURT
- ½ TSP SALT
- ½ TSP BLACK PEPPER
- 1 LEMON JUICE
- 2 TBSP OLIVE OIL
- LIME WEDGES

INSTRUCTIONS

- CUT THE 2 CHICKEN BREASTS AND LEGS, RUB THE SALT OVER THE CHICKEN. COMBINE RAS EL HANOUT, YOGURT, LEMON JUICE, AND SALT IN A LARGE BOWL.
- ADD CHICKEN AND COAT IT WELL.
- MARINATE THE CHICKEN FOR 2 HOURS
- PREHEAT THE GRILL OVER A MEDIUM HEAT OVEN 180° C.
- REMOVE CHICKEN FROM THE FRIDGE 30 MIN BEFORE COOKING.
- DRIZZLE OLIVE OIL AND COOK FOR 5 MINUTES UNTIL IT GETS A GOLDEN COLOR.
- FLIP THE SIDES AND COOK FOR ANOTHER 5 MINUTES
- TAKE A BAKING TRAY AND ROAST IN THE OVEN FOR 25 MINUTES UNTIL THE JUICES COME OUT.
- TAKE IT OUT AND LET IT REST IN THE FOIL FOR 10 MINUTES.
- SEASON WITH SALT AND LIME AND HAVE A JUICY DINNER!

KETO EYEBALL SPINACH

SERVING: 2 PERSONS
COOKING TIME: 20 MIN

CARBS: 23G
PROTEIN: 82G
FATS: 82G
FIBER: 5.2G
SODIUM: 2969MG
CALORIES: 1161 KCAL

INGREDIENTS

- 1 TBSP BUTTER
- 2 CUPS SPINACH
- ⅖ CUP WHIPPED CREAM
- 1 CUP MOZZARELLA CHEESE
- 4 EGGS
- 1 TBSP CHILI SAUCE
- 4 BLACK OLIVES
- 2 TSP GARLIC POWDER
- ½ TSP SALT
- ½ TSP BLACK PEPPER

INSTRUCTIONS

- PREHEAT THE OVEN TO 350°F. GREASE THE DISH WITH BUTTER.
- MIX CREAM, SPINACH, HALF MOZZARELLA, GARLIC POWDER, SALT, AND PEPPER IN A BOWL. MIX WITH CREAMY SPINACH AND LEAVE SPACE FOR EGGS.
- CRACK EGGS IN THE SPACES AND TOP WITH MOZZARELLA CHEESE. BAKE FOR 20 MINUTES.
- REMOVE THE DISH FROM THE OVEN AND ALLOW IT TO COOL.
- PUT BLACK OLIVES IN THE MIDDLE OF THE PUPIL. ENJOY YOUR SPOOKY EYE CASSEROLE!

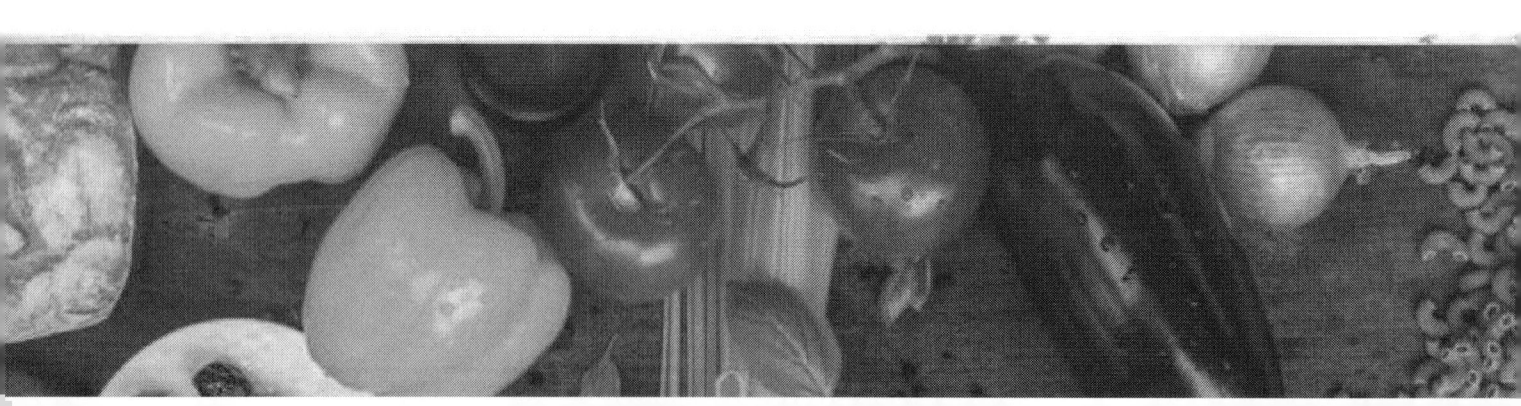

LEMON MERINGUE

SERVING: 4 PERSONS
COOKING TIME: 25 MIN

CARBS: 78G
PROTEIN: 57G
FATS: 47G
FIBER: 13G
SODIUM: 442MG
CALORIES: 1052KCAL

INGREDIENTS

- 5 WHOLE EGGS
- ½ CUP ZERO CARBS ARTIFICIAL SWEETENER
- ¼ CUP LEMON JUICE
- 1 CUP COCONUT FLOUR
- ½ TSP VANILLA ESSENCE

INSTRUCTIONS

- SEPARATE THE EGG YOLKS AND WHITES INTO SEPARATE BOWLS.
- BEAT UP THE EGG YOLKS FOR 1 MINUTE ANDADD SWEETENER TO IT. BEAT IT FOR 3-4 MINUTES UNTIL VOLUME DOUBLES.
- ADD IN COCONUT FLOUR GRADUALLY AND KEEP BEATING IT.
- THEN POUR IN LEMON JUICE AND VANILLA ESSENCE AND BEAT IT.
- SPREAD THE BATTER IN THE DEEP BAKING DISH AND BAKE IT AT 375° FOR 8-10 MINUTES.
- MEANWHILE, BEAT THE EGG WHITES UNTIL THE HARD PEAKS FORM.
- TAKE OUT THE BAKED EGG MIXTURE AND LAYER THE EGG WHITES.
- BAKE AT 350°F FOR 5 MINUTES AND ENJOY THE LOW CARB LEMON MERINGUE.

BAKED SQUASH WITH RICE

SERVING: 2 PERSONS
COOKING TIME: 30 MIN

CARBS: 46G
PROTEIN: 24G
FATS: 53G
FIBER: 14G
SODIUM: 2215MG
CALORIES: 713KCAL

INGREDIENTS

- 1 BUTTERNUT SQUASH
- 1 CUP CAULIFLOWER RICE
- SALT TO TASTE
- PEPPER TO TASTE
- ½ CUP CHEDDAR CHEESE
- ¼ CUP OLIVES
- ½ CUP MUSHROOMS
- 2 TBSP TOMATO PASTE
- 1 TSP GARLIC POWDER
- ½ TSP OREGANO
- 1 CUP CHICKEN BROTH
- 2 TBSP OLIVE OIL

INSTRUCTIONS

- CUT TWO BUTTERNUT SQUASH INTO HALVES. DESEED IT AND GIVE IT AN OLIVE OIL SPRAY.
- SEASON IT WITH SALT AND PEPPER. BAKE AT 400°F FOR 20 MINUTES.
- MEANWHILE, HEAT THE OLIVE OIL IN A PAN.
- ADD IN TOMATO PASTE. SAUTE FOR 30 SECONDS. ADD IN GARLIC POWDER AND RICE. ADD IN SALT, PEPPER, AND PUT IN MUSHROOMS AND OLIVES IN THE END. MIX THE WHOLE RICE BETTER EVENLY.
- TAKE OUT THE BAKED SQUASH AND REMOVE THE PULP AND DUMP IT IN THE RICE MIXTURE.
- STUFF THE SQUASH PEELS WITH THE RICE MIXTURE. TOP UP WITH CHEESE.
- SPRINKLE OREGANO ON THE TOP AND BAKE IT FOR 8-10 MINUTES AT 400°F. A COMPLETE KETO MEAL IS GOOD TO GO!

BAKED BACON EGGS

SERVING: 2 PERSONS
COOKING TIME: 20 MIN

CARBS: 31G
PROTEIN: 93G
FATS: 84G
FIBER: 6G
SODIUM: 2042MG
CALORIES: 1261KCAL

INGREDIENTS

- 16 BACON STRIPS
- 4 EGGS
- SALT TO TASTE
- PEPPER TO TASTE
- ½ CUP TOMATO PASTE

INSTRUCTIONS

- BRUSH THE BACON STRIPS WITH TOMATO PASTE ON ONE SIDE.
- SPRAY THE OLIVE OIL ON THE CUPCAKE TRAY.
- ARRANGE THE FOUR BACON PER CUPCAKE ALL AROUND THE FOUR SIDES KEEPING THE OTHER END HANGING OUTSIDE.
- CRACK AN EGG IN EACH BACON ALIGNED CUPCAKE.
- SPRINKLE SALT AND PEPPER IN THE END.
- POP IN THE OVEN FOR 12 MINUTES AT 350°F AND TAKE OUT THE CRISPY HOT PROTEIN PACKAGE.

PAIR IT WITH AVOCADO TO GET ALONG WITH FATS!

AVOCADO ALMOND CAKE

SERVING: 4 PERSONS
COOKING TIME: 30 MIN

CARBS: 120G
PROTEIN: 56G
FATS: 181G
FIBER: 45G
SODIUM: 1224MG
CALORIES: 2210KCAL

INGREDIENTS

FOR CAKE
- 1 RIPE AVOCADO
- 2 EGGS
- ½ CUP ALMOND MILK
- ¾ CUP ALMOND FLOUR
- ¼ CUP ERYTHRITOL
- ¼ CUP CREAM
- ½ TSP BAKING SODA

FOR ICING
- 1 AVOCADO
- ¼ CUP COCONUT CREAM
- 2 TBSP ZERO CARB SWEETENER
- ½ CUP FINELY CRUSHED ALMONDS

INSTRUCTIONS

- BLEND ONE AVOCADO, 2 EGGS, ALMOND MILK, CREAM IN A BLENDER.
- COMBINE THE ALMOND FLOUR, ERYTHRITOL, BAKING SODA IN A SEPARATE BOWL. MIX IT NICELY.
- NOW ADD IN AVOCADO BATTER IN DRY INGREDIENTS GRADUALLY AND KEEP STIRRING.
- SPREAD THE BATTER IN THE CAKE MOLD AND POP IN THE OVEN AT 400°F FOR 25 MINUTES.
- BLEND ONE AVOCADO, COCONUT CREAM, AND SWEETENER IN A BLENDER AND SPREAD IT ON THE CAKE.
- TOP UP WITH THE CRUSHED ALMONDS.

KETO PIZZA

SERVING: 4 PERSONS
COOKING TIME: 30 MIN

CARBS: 18G
PROTEIN: 105G
FATS: 170G
FIBER: 3.4G
SODIUM: 4478MG
CALORIES: 2019 KCAL

INGREDIENTS

FOR CRUST
- 4 EGGS
- 6 OZ CHEESE

FOR TOPPING
- 3 TBSP TOMATO SAUCE
- 1 TSP OREGANO
- 5 OZ. MOZZARELLA CHEESE
- 1 ½ OZ. PEPPERONI
- 5 BLACK OLIVES
- 2 OZ. LEAFY GREENS
- 3 TBSP OLIVE OIL
- ½ TSP SALT
- ½ TSP GROUND BLACK PEPPER

INSTRUCTIONS

- PREHEAT THE OVEN TO 400°F.
- MAKE THE CRUST, CRACK EGGS INTO A MEDIUM BOWL AND THEN ADD CHEESE. STIR IT TO GET COMBINED.
- USE A SPATULA AND SPREAD THE CHEESE AND ADD AN EGG TO THE BATTER.
- SPREAD THE DOUGH ON THE BAKING TRAY ALIGNED WITH PARCHMENT PAPER.
- POP IN THE OVEN FOR 15 MINUTES UNTIL THE PIZZA CRUST BECOMES GOLDEN BROWN. TAKE IT OUT OF THE OVEN AND LET IT COOL.
- SPREAD TOMATO SAUCE ON THE CRUST AND SPRINKLE OREGANO, CHEESE, PEPPERONI, AND BLACK OLIVES ON THE TOP.
- BAKE FOR 10 MINUTES AND TAKE IT OUT. SERVE A HOT SIZZLING PIZZA!

KETO CREAM PUFFS

SERVING: 4 PERSONS
COOKING TIME: 30 MIN

CARBS: 55G
PROTEIN: 45G
FATS: 81G
FIBER: 18G
SODIUM: 254MG
CALORIES: 1090KCAL

INGREDIENTS

- ¾ CUP ALMOND FLOUR
- ¼ CUP FLAX MEAL
- ½ CUP ARTIFICIAL SWEETENER
- 1 TBSP XANTHAN GUM
- 3 EGGS
- 4 TBSP MILK
- 1 CUP WHIPPED CREAM

INSTRUCTIONS

- COMBINE THE ALMOND FLOUR, FLAX MEAL, SWEETENER, XANTHAN GUM IN A BOWL.
- WHISK THE TWO EGGS AND ADD MILK IN IT.
- NOW MIX THE BEATEN EGGS IN THE DRY INGREDIENTS AND KEEP WHISKING TO AVOID LUMPS.
- PUT THE BATTER IN THE ICING BAG AND MAKE PUFFS ON THE BAKING TRAY.
- POP IN AT 375°F FOR 25 MINUTES.
- MAKE A HOLE ON THE BOTTOM OF THE PUFFS AND FILL IN THE WHIPPED CREAM WITH THE HELP OF AN ICING GUN.

STORE IN THE REFRIGERATOR AND PICK ONE WHEN CRAVING FOR THE CREAMY DESSERT!

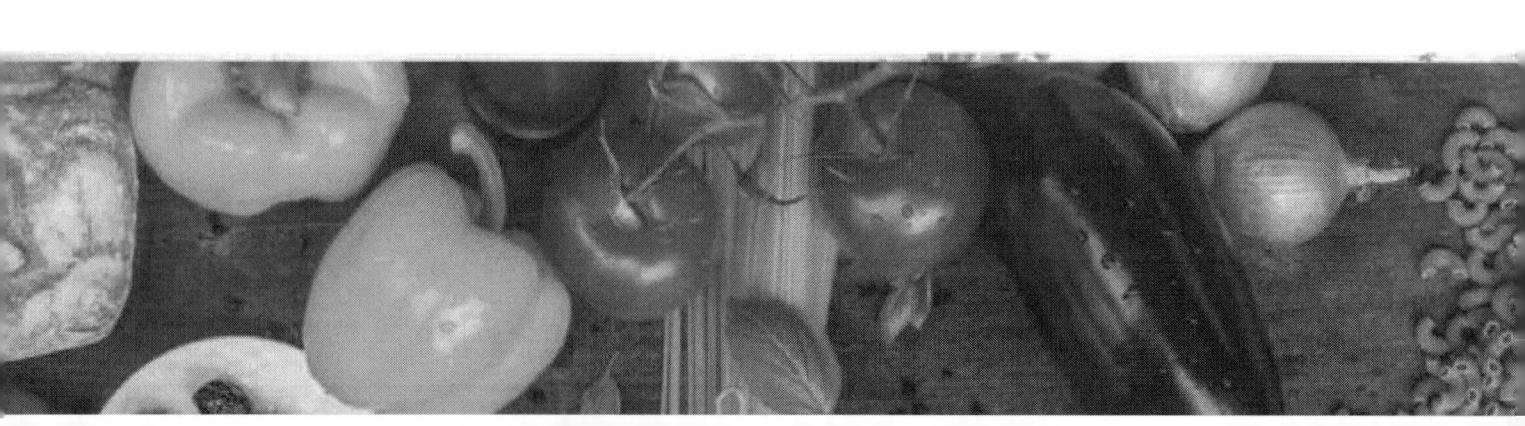

LEMON DELIGHT

SERVING: 2 PERSONS
COOKING TIME: 15 MIN

CARBS: 100G
PROTEIN: 25G
FATS: 123G
FIBER: 34G
SODIUM: 87MG
CALORIES: 1373 KCAL

INGREDIENTS

- 1 CUP COCONUT MILK
- 1 CUP ALMOND MILK
- ½ CUP HEAVY CREAM
- 1 TBSP ZERO CARB SWEETENER
- ½ CUP FLAX SEEDS
- 1 TSP LEMON JUICE

INSTRUCTIONS

- PREPARE AND GATHER ALL THE INGREDIENTS
- PUT-IN COCONUT MILK, ALMOND MILK, LEMON JUICE, FLAX SEEDS, AND STEVIA IN A BLENDER.
- COMBINE IT WELL
- POUR LEMON DESSERT INTO CUPS
- YOU CAN COVER WITH PLASTIC WRAP AND POP IN THE FRIDGE TO GET A CHILLED ONE. START YOUR DAY WITH A LEMON DESSERT!

PORCINI STEAK

SERVING: 2 PERSONS
COOKING TIME: 25 MIN

CARBS: 31G
PROTEIN: 45G
FATS: 123G
FIBER: 8G
SODIUM: 1271MG
CALORIES: 1372 KCAL

INGREDIENTS

- 2 TBSP DRIED PORCINI MUSHROOM
- 2 CLOVE GARLIC (CRUSHED)
- ½ TSP KOSHER SALT
- ½ TSP CAYENNE PEPPER
- 2 TBSP THYME LEAVES
- 100G UNSALTED BUTTER
- 1 LB BEEF STEAK
- 1 BUNCH SALAD ONION
- 2 LEMONS
- 1 TBSP OLIVE OIL

INSTRUCTIONS

- BOIL THE PORCINI IN WATER AND SET ASIDE TO DRAIN THEN ADD GARLIC, THYME, AND BUTTER.
- SEASON IT WITH KOSHER SALT AND CAYENNE PEPPER. STIR IT WHEN IT GETS COMBINED. SPREAD PORCINI ON THE STEAKS.
- PREHEAT THE LARGE FRYING PAN ON HIGH HEAT. MELT THE BUTTER AND COOK STEAKS FOR 2-3 MINUTES AND THEN COOK FOR 1-2 MINUTES UNDER MEDIUM HEAT.
- REMOVE THE STEAKS FROM THE PAN AND COVER WITH FOIL AND LEAVE IT FOR 4 MINUTES.
- COOK ONIONS AND LEMON HALVES IN THE OLIVE OIL AND COOK FOR EACH SIDE FOR 2 MINUTES UNTIL IT BECOMES SLIGHTLY SOFTENED.
- SERVE STEAKS WITH LEMON AND ONIONS OVER THE BUTTERED PORCINI!

TOMATO SANDWICHES

SERVING: 2 PERSONS
COOKING TIME: 20 MIN

CARBS: 24G
PROTEIN: 98G
FATS: 81G
FIBER: 3.6G
SODIUM: 2305MG
CALORIES: 1410KCAL

INGREDIENTS

- 2 TOMATOES
- 4 HAMS
- ½ CUP PARMESAN CHEESE
- ½ CUP MOZZARELLA CHEESE
- 1 TSP OREGANO
- 2 TBSP OLIVE OIL

INSTRUCTIONS

- CUT THE ½ INCH THICK CIRCULAR SLICES OF TOMATOES.
- PUT FOUR CIRCULAR SLICES OF TOMATOES IN THE BAKING TRAY.
- PLACE HAM ON IT. YOU CAN FOLD IT TO GET A BETTER FORM.
- PLACE THE OTHER FOUR TOMATO SLICES ON EACH HAM.
- NOW PUT IN A LOT OF CHEDDAR AND MOZZARELLA CHEESE ON THE TOP OF EACH TOMATO SANDWICH.
- SPRINKLE OREGANO IN THE END. DRIZZLE OLIVE OIL GENEROUSLY.
- BAKE AT 375°F FOR 8-10 MINUTES AND ENJOY THE HEALTHY SANDWICHES!

CHEESECAKE MUFFINS

SERVING: 2 PERSONS
COOKING TIME: 20 MIN

CARBS: 50G
PROTEIN: 40G
FATS: 226G
FIBER: 2.3G
SODIUM: 1641MG
CALORIES: 2355 KCAL

INGREDIENTS

- 8 OZ. CREAM CHEESE
- 2 EGGS
- 1 TBSP LEMON JUICE
- 1 TSP VANILLA EXTRACT
- ½ CUP ERYTHRITOL POWDER
- ⅓ CUP COCONUT FLOUR
- ¾ CUP CREAM

INSTRUCTIONS

- PREHEAT THE OVEN TO 350° F.
- TAKE A MUFFIN PAN AND LINE PARCHMENT SHEETS. YOU CAN ALSO USE A REGULAR MUFFIN TRAY.
- MAKE A CHEESECAKE MIXTURE BY BEATING THE CREAM CHEESE AND ERYTHRITOL. CONTINUE BEATING UNTIL IT GETS SMOOTHER.
- ADD EGG, LEMON JUICE, AND VANILLA EXTRACT
- BEAT IT AGAIN AND MAKE IT SMOOTHER.
- TAKE A SPOON AND LINE A CHEESECAKE MIXTURE INTO A MUFFIN TRAY.
- BAKE FOR 12-15 MINUTES UNTIL THE MUFFINS
- BECOME PUFFED UP.
- PLACE THE MUFFINS IN THE REFRIGERATOR FOR 15-20 MINUTES.
- MEANWHILE, BEAT HEAVY CREAM UNTIL THE SOFT PEAK FORMS.
- TAKE A SPOON AND PUT WHIPPED CREAM ON EACH CHEESECAKE MUFFIN.

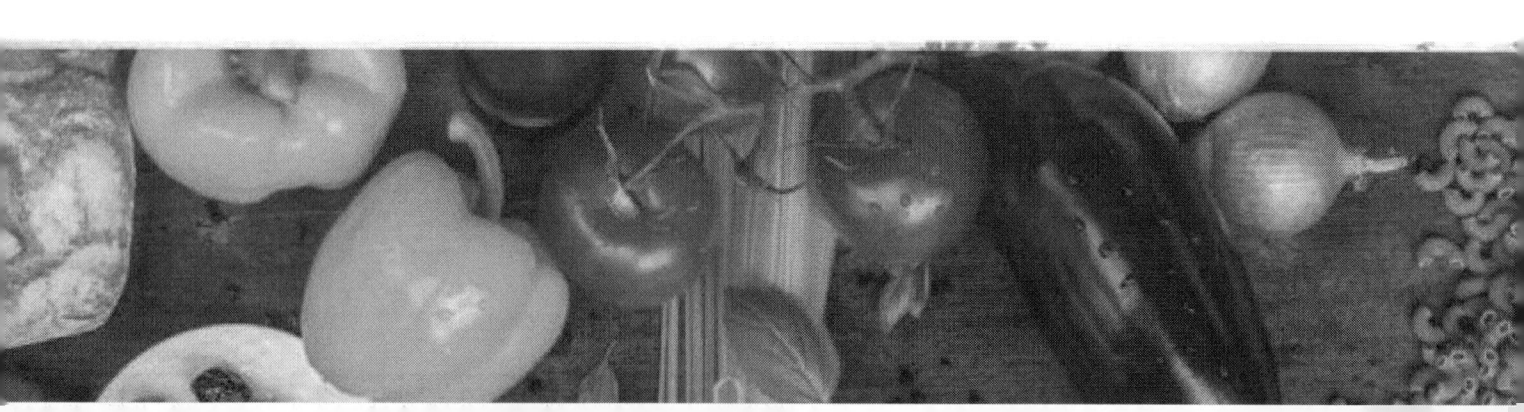

AVOCADO OMELET

SERVING: 2 PERSONS
COOKING TIME: 10 MIN

CARBS: 22G
PROTEIN: 30G
FATS: 76G
FIBER: 14G
SODIUM: 1758MG
CALORIES: 867 KCAL

INGREDIENTS

- 3 EGGS
- 2 TBSP BUTTER
- 1 OZ. CHEESE (SHREDDED)
- ¼ RED ONION
- 1 AVOCADO
- ½ TSP SALT
- ½ TSP BLACK PEPPER

INSTRUCTIONS

- CUT THE AVOCADO INTO SMALL PIECES AND CHOP THE ONION FINELY.
- CRACK THE EGGS. ADD SALT, PEPPER AND THEN WHISK IT WELL WITH THE FORK.
- MELT THE BUTTER IN A FRYING PAN. ADD-IN RED ONIONS, SLICED AVOCADO. SEASON WITH SALT AND PEPPER.
- COOK IT FOR 3-5 MINUTES UNTIL IT BECOMES SOFT AND STIR IT GENTLY.
- POUR EGG IN THE PAN AND MAKE SURE THAT IT FILLS THE SPACE BETWEEN THE ONIONS AND AVOCADO
- WHEN THE OMELET IS DONE, FLIP THE SIDE AND COOK IT FOR 2 MINUTES, THEN TOP WITH CHEESE OVER IT

STUFFED MUSHROOMS

SERVING: 4 PERSONS
COOKING TIME: 20 MIN

CARBS: 28G
PROTEIN: 64G
FATS: 93G
FIBER: 8.3G
SODIUM: 3131MG
CALORIES: 1181 KCAL

INGREDIENTS

- 4 BACON STRIPS
- 3 OZ. SPINACH
- 1 CLOVE GARLIC
- 4 OZ. CREAM CHEESE
- 1 EGG
- 2 TBSP ALMOND FLOUR
- ½ TSP SALT
- ½ TSP CAYENNE PEPPER
- 16 MEDIUM MUSHROOMS
- 1 CUP MOZZARELLA CHEESE

INSTRUCTIONS

- PREHEAT THE OVEN TO 350°F. COOK THE BACON BY USING A SKILLET, AND UNTIL IT GETS CRISPY. AFTER COOKING, PUT ASIDE AND LET IT COOL.
- SHIFT THE BACON INTO A LARGE BOWL.
- CRUMBLE THE BACON, THEN ADD SPINACH, GARLIC, CREAM CHEESE, EGG, ALMOND FLOUR, AND MOZZARELLA CHEESE AND MIX IT WELL.
- DON'T FORGET TO SEASON WITH SALT AND CAYENNE PEPPER. COMBINE THE INGREDIENTS THOROUGHLY.
- REMOVE THE STEMS OF THE MUSHROOMS AND STUFF THE MUSHROOM CAP WITH THE FILLING AND PLACE IT IN A BAKING DISH.
- BAKE AT 350°F FOR 20 MINUTES UNTIL THE CHEESE IS BROWNED AND START BUBBLING!

NO-BAKE CUPCAKES

SERVING: 4 PERSONS
COOKING TIME: 15 MIN

CARBS: 111G
PROTEIN: 31G
FATS: 120G
FIBER: 14G
SODIUM: 449MG
CALORIES: 1284 KCAL

INGREDIENTS

- ¼ CUP COCONUT BUTTER
- ⅓ CUP ZERO CARB SWEETENER
- ½ CUP ALMOND BUTTER
- ½ TSP VANILLA EXTRACT
- ¼ CUP MILK
- ½ CUP UNSWEETENED CHOCOLATE

INSTRUCTIONS

- TAKE A CUPCAKE TRAY AND LINE WITH A PARCHMENT PAPER
- TAKE A PAN AND HEAT COCONUT BUTTER, ZERO CARB SWEETENER, ALMOND BUTTER, AND VANILLA EXTRACT.
- HEAT THE MIXTURE ON LOW MEDIUM HEAT, STIR, CONTINUE TO MAKE A THICK PASTE AND THERE SHOULD BE NO LUMPS.
- DISTRIBUTE THIS BUTTER MIXTURE EQUALLY IN THE CUPCAKE TRAY.
- LET IT COOL DOWN IN THE REFRIGERATOR FOR HALF AN HOUR.
- MELT THE CHOCOLATE WITH MILK IN THE MICROWAVE FOR 30 SECONDS INTERVALS UNTIL IT BECOMES SMOOTH IN ITS CONSISTENCY
- DISTRIBUTE THE CHOCOLATE LAYER ON THE TOP OF THE ALMOND BUTTER LAYER
- PLACE THE CUPCAKE IN THE REFRIGERATOR FOR 30 MINUTES AND ENJOY NO-BAKE LAYERED CUPCAKES!

PORK & CABBAGE SALAD

SERVING: 2 PERSONS
COOKING TIME: 30 MIN

CARBS: 51G
PROTEIN: 135G
FATS: 105G
FIBER: 15G
SODIUM: 4986MG
CALORIES: 1678 KCAL

INGREDIENTS

- 16 OZ PORK CUBES
- 2 TBSP OLIVE OIL
- 2 TBSP SOY SAUCE
- 2 GARLIC CLOVES (MINCED)
- 1 TSP GINGER PASTE
- ½ ONION (THINLY SLICED)
- 24 OZ GREEN CABBAGE (THINLY SLICED)
- 1 TBSP VINEGAR
- ½ TSP SALT
- ½ TSP PEPPER
- ½ CUP CHOPPED GREEN ONION

INSTRUCTIONS

- TAKE A PAN AND HEAT OVER MEDIUM FLAME, ADD OLIVE OIL AND SAUTE PORK SHORTCUTS UNTIL IT IS PROPERLY COOKED.
- ADD SOY SAUCE, GARLIC, GINGER, AND ONION, AND THEN COOK FOR 4-5 MINUTES. ONCE COOKED, CHOP THEM INTO SMALLER CUBES WITH A SPATULA
- ADD CABBAGE, AND VINEGAR TO THE PAN AND STIR THE CABBAGE UNTIL IT BECOMES TENDER.
- SEASON WITH SALT AND PEPPER AND EAT HEALTHILY!

BACON CHIPS

SERVING: 2 PERSONS
COOKING TIME: 20 MIN

CARBS: 1.5G
PROTEIN: 23G
FATS: 40G
FIBER: 0G
SODIUM: 367MG
CALORIES: 457 KCAL

INGREDIENTS

- ½ CUP SWISS CHEESE (SHREDDED)
- ½ CHEDDAR CHEESE (SHREDDED)
- ⅛ CUP BACON (COOKED)
- 1 TBSP OLIVE OIL

INSTRUCTIONS

- PREHEAT THE OVEN TO 300°F. LINE A PARCHMENT PAPER AND SPRAY OLIVE OIL.
- SPREAD THE SWISS CHEESE OVER PARCHMENT PAPER.
- SPRINKLE BACON ON TOP OF SWISS CHEESE AND THEN LAYER WITH CHEDDAR CHEESE AS A FINAL LAYER
- SHAPE UP THE CHEESE LIKE A BIG RECTANGLE.
- BAKE IN THE OVEN FOR 10-12 MINUTES UNTIL THE CHEESE STARTS TO MELT AND BACON TURNS TO BROWN.
- LET IT COOL AND CUT INTO TRIANGLE-SHAPED CHIPS FROM A BIG RECTANGLE.

LET'S EAT A CRUNCHY SNACK!

KETO HAZELNUT SPREAD

SERVING: 4 PERSONS
COOKING TIME: 20 MIN

CARBS: 169G
PROTEIN: 42G
FATS: 186G
FIBER: 28G
SODIUM: 0.4MG
CALORIES: 1957 KCAL

INGREDIENTS

- 2 CUP HAZELNUTS
- ½ CUP ZERO CARB SWEETENER
- ¼ CUP COCOA POWDER
- 2 TBSP RAPESEED OIL
- 1 TSP VANILLA EXTRACT

INSTRUCTIONS

- PREHEAT THE OVEN TO 400° DEGREES F. LINE PARCHMENT PAPER ON THE BAKING DISH.
- SPREAD HAZELNUTS AND THEN ROAST IN THE OVEN FOR 8-10 MINUTES UNTIL IT GETS BROWN
- ALLOW IT TO COOL AND PLACE HAZELNUTS IN A STABLE CONTAINER AND CLOSE THE LID AND SHAKE IT WELL.
- REPEAT THE PROCESS UNTIL THE SKINS HAVE BEEN REMOVED FROM THE NUTS. YOU CAN ALSO RUB THE SKIN BY YOURSELF
- NOW BLEND THE NUTS FOR 2-3 MINUTES UNTIL IT FORMS A NUT BUTTER.
- ADD SWEETENER, COCOA POWDER, RAPESEED OIL, AND VANILLA EXTRACT AND BLEND IT WELL. BLEND FOR 1-2 MINUTES UNTIL IT BECOMES A SMOOTH SPREAD.
- STORE IN AN AIRTIGHT CONTAINER TO ENJOY THIS GLOSSY SMOOTH SPREAD!

CUCUMBER PICKLE

SERVING: 2 PERSONS
COOKING TIME: 10 MIN

CARBS: 53G
PROTEIN: 3G
FATS: 2.5G
FIBER: 4.2G
SODIUM: 1212MG
CALORIES: 118 KCAL

INGREDIENTS

- 6 OZ. CUCUMBER
- ½ CUP WATER
- ½ CUP VINEGAR
- ¼ CUP ERYTHRITOL
- ½ TSP RED PEPPER FLAKES
- ½ TSP CAYENNE PEPPER
- ½ TBSP CHIA SEEDS
- 2 TBSP ONIONS (CHOPPED)
- ½ TSP SALT
- ½ TSP PEPPER

INSTRUCTIONS

- CUT THE CUCUMBER INTO THIN SLICES
- ADD ALL THE INGREDIENTS TO THE CONTAINER AND SEAL IT TIGHTLY
- STORE IT FOR 12 HOURS AND ENJOY SWEET AND SOUR CUCUMBERS WHENEVER YOU WANT!

KETO TACO SOUP

SERVING: 4 PERSONS
COOKING TIME: 15 MIN

CARBS: 85G
PROTEIN: 150G
FATS: 234G
FIBER: 22G
SODIUM: 2482MG
CALORIES: 3034 KCAL

INGREDIENTS

FOR SOUP
- 16 OZ. BEEF
- 1 TBSP ALMOND OIL
- 1 MEDIUM ONION
- 3 GARLIC CLOVES
- 1 GREEN BELL PEPPER
- 10 OZ. TOMATOES
- 1 CUP HEAVY CREAM
- 2 TBSP TACO SEASONING
- ½ TSP SALT
- ½ TSP PEPPER
- 1 CUP BROTH

FOR GARNISHING
- 1 MEDIUM AVOCADO
- 4 TBSP SOUR CREAM
- 2 TBSP CILANTRO

INSTRUCTIONS

- DICE ONION, TOMATOES, AND BELL PEPPER IN A BOWL.
- TAKE A POT AND ADD ALMOND OIL, ONIONS, GARLIC, AND BEEF. LET IT COOK ON MEDIUM HEAT.
- SEASON WITH SALT AND PEPPER.
- WHEN THE BEEF IS BROWNED THEN, ADD BELL PEPPER AND DICED TOMATOES, CREAM, AND TACO SEASONING
- STIR ALL THE INGREDIENTS TOGETHER.
- ADD BEEF BROTH AND BRING THE SOUP TO BOIL
- ONCE BOIL, THEN REDUCE THE HEAT AND SIMMER FOR 10-15 MINUTES AND ADJUST THE CONSISTENCY.
- GARNISH WITH AVOCADOS, CREAM, AND CILANTRO. SQUEEZE LIME JUICE FOR A SUPERB TASTE!

COATED MOZZARELLA PEARLS

SERVING: 2 PERSONS
COOKING TIME: 30 MIN

CARBS: 28G
PROTEIN: 56G
FATS: 73G
FIBER: 13G
SODIUM: 5943MG
CALORIES: 966 KCAL

INGREDIENTS

- 1 TSP OLIVE OIL
- ¼ TSP RED VINEGAR
- 1 GARLIC CLOVE (MINCED)
- ½ TSP SALT
- ½ TSP BLACK PEPPER
- 1 TSP SEASONING (HERBS, THYME, ROSEMARY, BASIL, AND PARSLEY)
- 1 LEMON ZEST
- 1 ARTICHOKE
- 8 OZ. MOZZARELLA PEARLS
- ½ CUP OF GREEN OLIVES

FOR TOPPING
- PISTACHIOS AND CASHEWS (CHOPPED)

INSTRUCTIONS

- HEAT THE NON-STICK FRYING PAN AND THEN ADD OLIVE OIL ON MEDIUM HEAT.
- CUT THE ARTICHOKES INTO SMALL PIECES
- TAKE A BOWL AND ADD ARTICHOKES, MOZZARELLA PEARLS MINCED GARLIC, SEASONING, HERBS, LEMON, AND BLACK PEPPER
- MARINATE IT WELL AND LEAVE IT FOR 30 MINUTES
- PUT IN THE FRYING PAN AND COOK FOR 3-5 MINUTES
- TOSS IT UNTIL IT IS COOKED COMPLETELY
- DRIZZLE LEMON AND CHOPPED CASHEWS AND PISTACHIOS ON TOP AND IT IS READY TO GO!

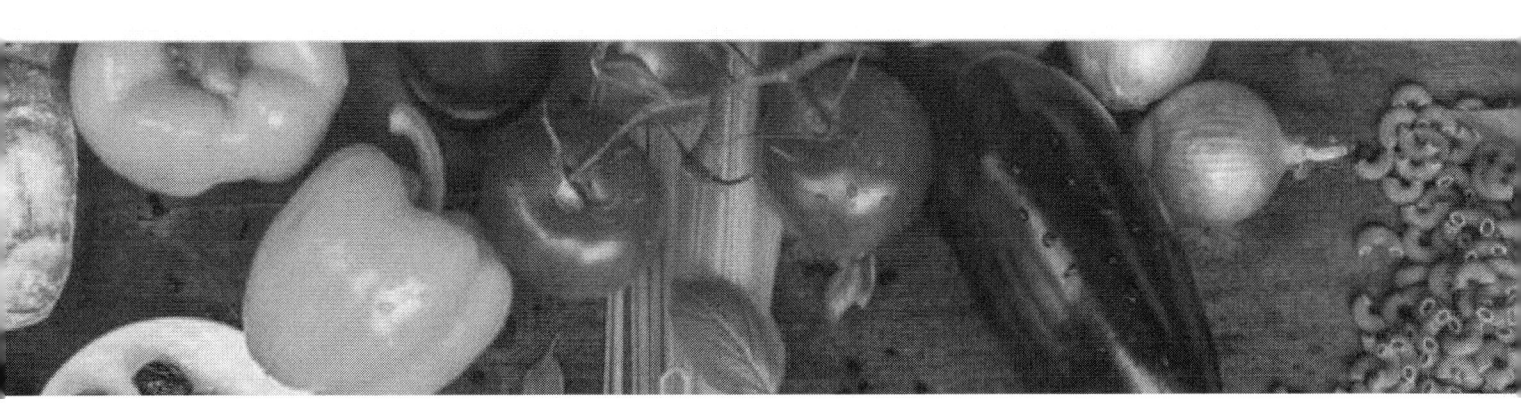

HALLOUMI SPINACH

SERVING: 2 PERSONS
COOKING TIME: 15 MIN

CARBS: 84G
PROTEIN: 88G
FATS: 65G
FIBER: 3G
SODIUM: 3048MG
CALORIES: 1260 KCAL

INGREDIENTS

- 10 OZ. HALLOUMI CHEESE
- 1 CUP PLAIN GREEK YOGURT
- ¼ CUP MINT (CHOPPED)
- 2 TSP GARLIC (CHOPPED)
- ½ TSP SALT
- ½ TSP PEPPER
- 10 OZ BOILED SPINACH

INSTRUCTIONS

- TAKE A BOWL AND COMBINE GREEK YOGURT, FRESH MINT, GARLIC, OLIVE OIL, SALT, AND PEPPER. STIR UNTIL COMBINED WELL.
- PUT THE HALLOUMI CHEESE INTO THE PAN WITHOUT ADDING ANY OIL.
- FRY ON MEDIUM HEAT FOR 2-4 MINUTES. TO MAKE SURE THAT THE CHEESE IS COOKED.
- FLIP THE HALLOUMI CHEESE UNTIL IT IS GOLDEN BROWN.
- PUT GREENS IN A BOWL AND THEN ADD YOGURT TO IT. TOP UP WITH FRIED HALLOUMI CHEESE ON THE TOP.

KETO STUFFED CREPES

SERVING: 2 PERSONS
COOKING TIME: 20 MIN

CARBS: 67G
PROTEIN: 111G
FATS: 202G
FIBER: 2.1G
SODIUM: 2742MG
CALORIES: 2531 KCAL

INGREDIENTS

FOR CREPES
- 8 OZ CHEESE
- 6 MEDIUM EGGS
- ½ TSP CAYENNE POWDER
- 1 TBSP BROWN SUGAR
- 2 TBSP BUTTER

FOR STUFFING
- 6 OZ CREAM CHEESE
- 1 CUP MILK
- ½ TAP LEMON
- 1 TSP VANILLA EXTRACT
- ½ TSP HONEY

INSTRUCTIONS

- TAKE A BLENDER AND ADD IN CREPES, EGGS, CAYENNE POWDER, SUGAR AND BLEND IT WELL.
- LEAVE THE BATTER FOR 5 MINUTES, TILL THEN HEAT THE FRYING PAN ON A MEDIUM HEAT
- ADD BUTTER AND LET IT MELT. POUR BATTER INTO THE PAN AND MAKE 6 ROUND-SHAPED CREPE
- COOK FOR 3-5 MINUTES
- FLIP THE SIDES AND LET IT COOK FOR ANOTHER 2 MINUTES
- REPEAT THE PROCESS UNTIL 8 CREPES ARE PREPARED
- LATER, TAKE A BOWL AND ADD CREAM CHEESE, MILK, LEMON, VANILLA EXTRACT, AND HONEY. COMBINE THE INGREDIENTS
- SMEAR CREPE, FILL THE MIDDLE OF THE CREPE AND THEN FOLD IT TO MAKE A ROLL. REPEAT THE PROCESS 7 TIMES
- SERVE WITH CRUSHED NUTS ON THE TOP!

CHICKEN CABBAGE DISH

SERVING: 2 PERSONS
COOKING TIME: 15 MIN

CARBS: 18G
PROTEIN: 129G
FATS: 134G
FIBER: 5G
SODIUM: 3590MG
CALORIES: 1781 KCAL

INGREDIENTS

- 1 LB CHICKEN STRIPS
- 1 CUP SHREDDED CABBAGE
- 1 TSP ONION POWDER
- 1 TSP GARLIC POWDER
- ½ CUP MAYONNAISE
- 4 TBSP CREAM
- 2 TSP LEMON JUICE
- 1 TBSP DIJON MUSTARD
- ½ TSP SALT
- ½ TSP BLACK PEPPER
- ½ CUP ALMOND FLOUR
- 4 TBSP OLIVE OIL

INSTRUCTIONS

- MARINATE THE CHICKEN STRIPS WITH LEMON JUICE, ONION POWDER, GARLIC POWDER, MUSTARD, SALT, AND BLACK PEPPER.
- FOLD THE CHICKEN IN ALMOND FLOUR AND COOK IT IN OLIVE OIL FOR 8-10 MINUTES.
- PUT THE SHREDDED CABBAGE IN A BOWL. ADD MAYONNAISE AND CREAM TO IT.
- SPRINKLE SALT AND BLACK PEPPER OVER IT. MIX IT WELL.
- DISH OUT THE CHICKEN AND SERVE IT WITH CREAMY CABBAGE.

ALMOND GNOCCHI ROLLS

SERVING: 4 PERSONS
COOKING TIME: 20 MIN

CARBS: 66G
PROTEIN: 74G
FATS: 272G
FIBER: 31G
SODIUM: 2160MG
CALORIES: 2887 KCAL

INGREDIENTS

GNOCCHI DOUGH
- 2 CUPS ALMOND FLOUR
- ¼ CUP BUTTER
- ½ CUP MOZZARELLA CHEESE
- ½ CUP MILK
- 1 LARGE EGG

FOR SAUCE
- ½ CUP BUTTER
- 1 TSP LEMON ZEST
- 1 TSP THYME LEAVES

INSTRUCTIONS

- MAKE A DOUGH BY ADDING ALMOND FLOUR, BUTTER, MILK, AND EGG. MIX IT WELL AND KNEAD IT CONTINUOUSLY UNTIL THE PERFECT DOUGH IS NOT FORMED.
- MICROWAVE BUTTER AND MOZZARELLA CHEESE AND COMBINE IT WELL.
- BOIL GNOCCHI FOR 2 MINUTES AND THEN LET IT DRY
- COOK GNOCCHI FOR 5 MINUTES, THEN FILL THE DOUGH
- MAKE LONG ROLLS OF DOUGH AND CUT INTO BITE-SIZE SHAPE AND PUT IN THE FRIDGE FOR 15 MINUTES BEFORE COOKING
- TAKE IT OUT AND COOK FOR 5-6 MINUTES UNTIL THE COLOR GETS GOLDEN BROWN. PUT ASIDE WHEN IT IS COOKED.
- TAKE ANOTHER PAN AND MAKE THE SAUCE BY ADDING BUTTER, LEMON ZEST, THYME AND COOK FOR 2 MINUTES
- COAT GNOCCHI ROLLS WITH SAUCE AND STIR IT GENTLY AND SERVE IT ON A PLATE!

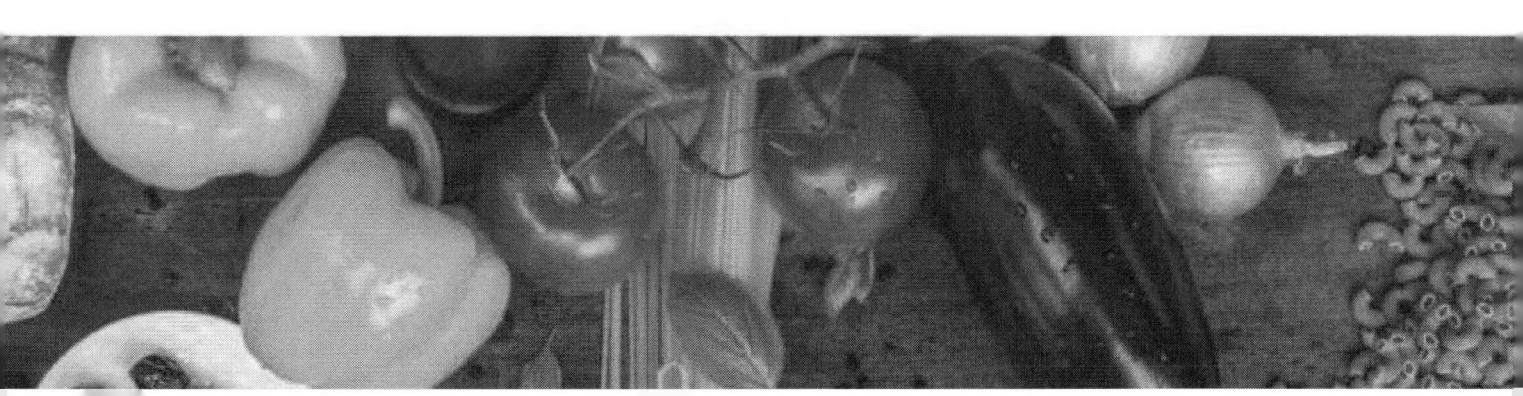

EGG TART

SERVING: 2 PERSONS
COOKING TIME: 15 MIN

CARBS: 41G
PROTEIN: 50G
FATS: 48G
FIBER: 11G
SODIUM: 2115MG
CALORIES: 774KCAL

INGREDIENTS

- 4 EGGS
- 1 MEDIUM ONION
- 1 MEDIUM TOMATO
- 1 CUP RAW SPINACH
- 1 CUP ZUCCHINI
- 1 CUP BROCCOLI
- 1 TSP KOSHER SALT
- 1 TSP BLACK PEPPER
- ½ CUP CHEESE
- ½ CUP WHIP CREAM

INSTRUCTIONS

- SHRED ALL THE VEGETABLES AND SEASON WITH SALT AND PEPPER
- MIX IT WELL AND LINE IN A GREASE TART PAN. YOU NEED TO COVER THE SIDES AND TART THE FILLING COMPLETELY
- BAKE IT FOR 15 MINUTES AT 350°F.
- CRACK THE EGGS AND BEAT WITH BROCCOLI, ZUCCHINI, SPINACH, ONION, TOMATO, CREAM, AND CHEESE.
- NOW BAKE THE TART FOR ANOTHER 15 MINUTES. YOUR HEALTHY BREAKFAST IS READY

BAKED EGGS

SERVING: 4 PERSONS
COOKING TIME: 15 MIN

CARBS: 50G
PROTEIN: 36G
FATS: 82G
FIBER: 7.2G
SODIUM: 2456MG
CALORIES: 1068 KCAL

INGREDIENTS

- 4 OZ PANCETTA
- 4 EGGS
- ½ CUP RED ONION (CHOPPED)
- ½ CUP CHOPPED ONION
- 2 TSP OREGANO
- 2 TBSP BASIL LEAVES
- 1 CUP ALMOND MILK
- ⅔ CUP PARMESAN CHEESE
- 1 TSP GARLIC POWDER
- ½ TSP SALT
- ½ TSP BLACK PEPPER
- ½ CUP TOMATOES (CHOPPED)
- 1 TSP TOMATO SAUCE
- RED CHILI FLAKES (GARNISHED)

INSTRUCTIONS

- PREHEAT THE OVEN TO 425°F. CHOP AND DICE ONION AND TOMATO. SHRED THE PARMESAN CHEESE AND MINCE THE GARLIC. ADD IN OREGANO AND BASILS IN THE SAME BOWL.
- ADD IN THE PAN AND FRY FOR 2 MINUTES UNTIL IT BECOMES TENDER. REMOVE THE MIXTURE FROM THE PAN, THEN ADD ALMOND MILK AND PARMESAN CHEESE, AND MIX IT.
- STIR GARLIC, SEA SALT, PEPPER, TOMATO SAUCE, AND ONION. ADD EGG IN EACH CREVICE.
- PLACE IN THE OVEN AND COOK FOR 20 MINUTES UNTIL THE SIDES GET GOLDEN BROWN. GARNISH PARSLEY AND RED CHILI FLAKES OVER IT. YOUR DINNER IS READY!

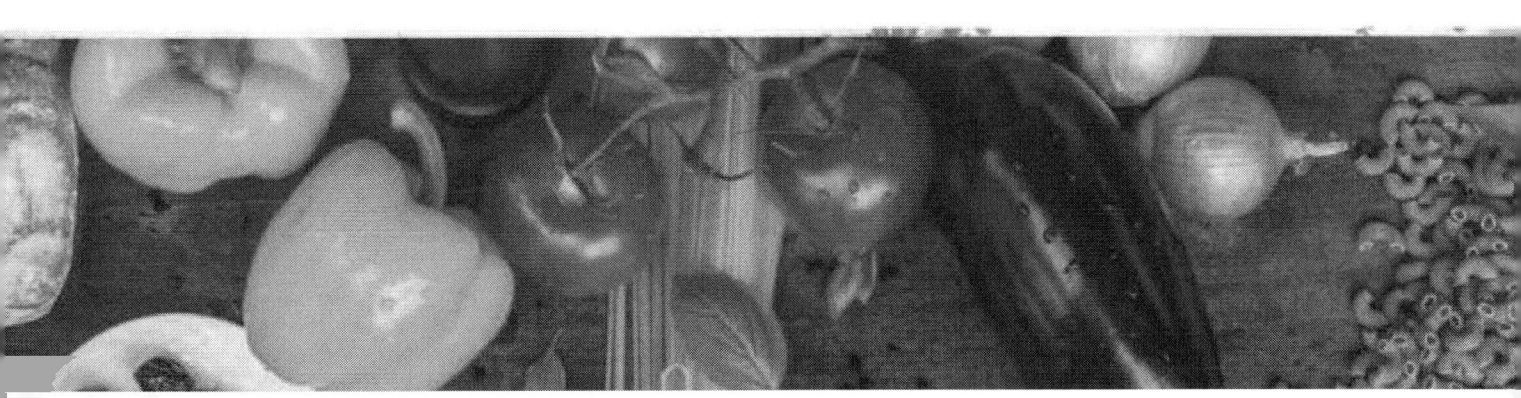

ROASTED SALMON

SERVING: 2 PERSONS
COOKING TIME: 10 MIN

CARBS: 16G
PROTEIN: 62G
FATS: 86G
FIBER: 5.8G
SODIUM: 1351MG
CALORIES: 1087 KCAL

INGREDIENTS

- 8 OZ ASPARAGUS SPEARS
- 4 TBSP COCONUT OIL
- 9 OZ SALMON
- ½ TSP SEA SALT
- ½ TSP CAYENNE PEPPER
- ½ SMALL ORANGE

INSTRUCTIONS

- CLEAN THE ASPARAGUS SPEAR AND THEN CUT THE SPEARS AT THE BOTTOM.
- ADD THE COCONUT OIL TO THE FRYING PAN AND THEN HEAT ON A MEDIUM FLAME.
- FRY ASPARAGUS FOR 5-6 MINUTES UNTIL IT IS COOKED, MAKE SURE IT DOESN'T BECOME SOFT.
- ADD THE REMAINING COCONUT OIL TO THE PAN AND THEN ADD SALMON.
- SEASON IT WITH SALT AND CAYENNE PEPPER.
- COOK BOTH SIDES OF THE SALMON UNTIL IT IS COMPLETELY COOKED AND STIR ASPARAGUS PERIODICALLY
- SERVE ON A PLATE AND YOUR DELICIOUS MEAL IS READY!

ZUCCHINI BEEF LASAGNA

SERVING: 2 PERSONS
COOKING TIME: 25 MIN

CARBS: 29G
PROTEIN: 172G
FATS: 130G
FIBER: 5G
SODIUM: 2465MG
CALORIES: 1999 KCAL

INGREDIENTS

FOR SAUCE
- 1 LB BEEF
- 1 TSP THYME
- 1 TSP ALFREDO SAUCE

RICOTTA MIXTURE
- 1 ZUCCHINI RAW
- ¼ CUP MOZZARELLA CHEESE
- ¼ CUP PARMESAN
- ¼ CUP RICOTTA CHEESE
- 1 TBSP WHIP CREAM
- ½ TSP ITALIAN SEASONING
- 1 CUP CAULIFLOWER RICE
- 2 EGGS
- 1 TSP GARLIC POWDER
- ½ TSP SALT
- ½ BLACK PEPPER

INSTRUCTIONS

- PREHEAT THE OVEN TO 375 °F. CUT THE ZUCCHINI INTO SMALL CUBES AND COOK FOR 3-5 MINUTES UNTIL IT GETS BROWN
- TAKE A BOWL AND ADD IN ZUCCHINI CUBES, EGGS, MOZZARELLA CHEESE, CAULIFLOWER RICE, PARMESAN, AND ITALIAN SEASONING.
- SPREAD THE MIXTURE IN A BAKING TRAY LIKE A THICK SHEET
- COOK FOR 15 MINUTES UNTIL IT BECOMES BROWN
- SET THE BEEF SAUCE ON THE TOP
- MIX RICOTTA CHEESE, WHIP CREAM, AND PARMESAN, SALT, PEPPER, AND SPREAD OVER IT.

CHICKEN BALLS

SERVING: 4 PERSONS
COOKING TIME: 15 MIN

CARBS: 55G
PROTEIN: 133G
FATS: 128G
FIBER: 14G
SODIUM: 4537MG
CALORIES: 1980 KCAL

INGREDIENTS

- 1 LB CHICKEN (BONELESS, MINCED)
- 1 LARGE EGG
- ⅓ CUP ALMOND FLOUR
- 1 TSP KOSHER SALT
- ¼ TSP BLACK PEPPER
- ½ TSP GARLIC POWDER
- 1 DRIED PARSLEY
- 1 TBSP OLIVE OIL

FOR SAUCE
- 2 TBSP OLIVE OIL
- ½ CUP ONION (SLICED)
- 1 CUP YELLOW AND RED BELL PEPPER
- 2 CLOVE GARLIC
- ½ CUP WHITE WINE
- 1 CUP TOMATOES (CHOPPED)
- 1 CUP CHICKEN BROTH
- 1 TBSP CAPERS
- 1 TSP OREGANO
- ½ CUP PARMESAN

INSTRUCTIONS

- TAKE A MEDIUM BOWL AND ADD IN CHICKEN MINCE, EGG, ALMOND FLOUR, KOSHER SALT, BLACK PEPPER, GARLIC POWDER, AND DRIED PARSLEY.
- HEAT THE FRYING PAN AND ADD OLIVE OIL TO IT. MAKE 8 BALLS AND COOK IN THE FRYING PAN FOR 5 MINUTES.
- COOK UNTIL IT GETS BROWN COLOR AND PUT ASIDE.
- MAKE THE SAUCE BY HEATING ANOTHER FRYING PAN AND THEN ADD OLIVE OIL, ONION, YELLOW AND RED BELL PEPPERS, CHOPPED GARLIC, TOMATOES, CHICKEN BROTH, CAPERS, OREGANO, CHICKEN BROTH, AND COOK FOR 5 MINUTES
- DRIZZLE WHITE WINE OVER CHICKEN BALLS, ALONG WITH YUMMY SAUCE!

BAKED AVOCADO

SERVING: 1 PERSONS
COOKING TIME: 25 MIN

CARBS: 19G
PROTEIN: 11G
FATS: 48G
FIBER: 14G
SODIUM: 841MG
CALORIES: 518 KCAL

INGREDIENTS

- 1 AVOCADO
- 1 LARGE EGG
- 1 TBSP OLIVE OIL
- 1 TSP SALT
- 1 TSP CAYENNE PEPPER
- 1 TSP RED VINEGAR
- ½ CUP MOZZARELLA CHEESE

INSTRUCTIONS

- CUT AVOCADO INTO TWO HALVES AND REMOVE THE SEED. BREAK THE EGG IN THE MIDDLE HALF OF AVOCADO, THEN SPRINKLE SALT, PEPPER, CHEESE, AND RED VINEGAR ON THE TOP
- GREASE THE BAKING TRAY WITH OLIVE OIL AND LET IT BAKE FOR 15-18 MINUTES AT 375°F. BAKE UNTIL IT GETS GOLDEN BROWN COLOR.
- MAKE SURE WHEN IT IS COOKED, TAKE IT OUT AND TOP WITH CHEESE, AND PUT IN THE OVEN FOR ANOTHER 1-2 MINUTES.
- NOW YOU CAN ENJOY YOUR DAY!

COCONUT BREAD

SERVING: 4 PERSONS
COOKING TIME: 30 MIN

CARBS: 20G
PROTEIN: 23G
FATS: 61G
FIBER: 14G
SODIUM: 2763MG
CALORIES: 687 KCAL

INGREDIENTS

- 1 CUP COCONUT FLOUR
- 1 TSP YEAST
- ½ TSP SALT
- 1 LARGE EGG
- ½ TSP BAKING POWDER
- ½ TSP FLAX SEEDS
- ¼ CUP ALMOND
- ¼ CUP CASHEW
- 1 TSP RED VINEGAR
- ½ TSP AVOCADO OIL

INSTRUCTIONS

- PREPARE COCONUT BREAD BY TAKING A LARGE BOWL AND THEN ADD COCONUT FLOUR, SALT, BAKING POWDER, YEAST, GROUND FLAX SEEDS, AND CRUSHED NUTS.
- COMBINE ALL THE INGREDIENTS COMPLETELY AND THEN ADD AVOCADO OIL
- MIX VINEGAR IN 2 CUPS OF HOT WATER AND THEN FOLD THE DRY INGREDIENTS
- KEEP ADDING THE VINEGAR UNTIL THE SOFT DOUGH IS FORMED.
- STORE DOUGH IN THE HOT TOWEL AND LEAVE IT FOR AN HOUR.
- LINE A BAKING TRAY WITH PARCHMENT PAPER.
- GREASE IT WITH AVOCADO OIL AND THEN SPREAD THE DOUGH GENTLY.
- BAKE FOR 30 MINUTES AT 375°F IN THE OVEN AND WAIT FOR IT UNTIL THE DOUGH TURNS GOLDEN BROWN.
- SPRINKLE ROSEMARY OVER IT AND ENJOY YOUR BREAKFAST!

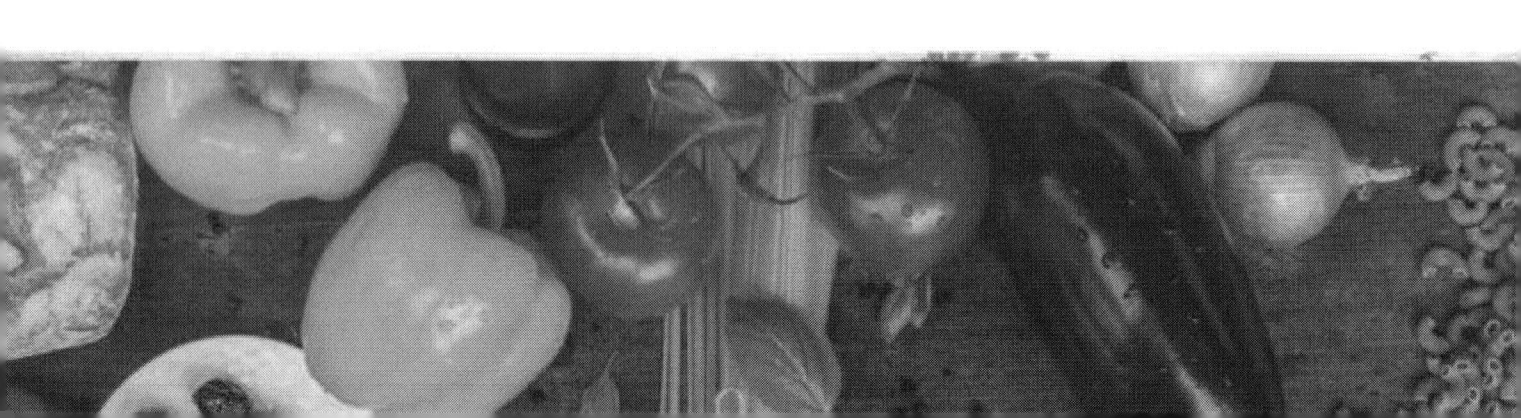

BROCCOLI FRITTERS

SERVING: 2 PERSONS
COOKING TIME: 15 MIN

CARBS: 40G
PROTEIN: 50G
FATS: 92G
FIBER: 17G
SODIUM: 1451MG
CALORIES: 1133 KCAL

INGREDIENTS

- ½ CUP BROCCOLI
- ½ CUP PARMESAN CHEESE
- 1 CUP ALMOND FLOUR
- ½ TSP GARLIC POWDER
- 2 SMALL EGGS
- ½ TSP KOSHER SALT
- ½ TSP CAYENNE PEPPER
- ½ TSP SESAME SEEDS
- ½ TSP BAKING POWDER
- ¼ TSP LEMON JUICE
- ½ TSP VINEGAR
- 1 TBSP COCONUT OIL

INSTRUCTIONS

- TAKE A POT AND BOIL BROCCOLI FOR 2 MINUTES UNTIL IT IS COOKED
- DRAIN IT AND CHOP BROCCOLI INTO MEDIUM-SIZED SHAPED
- TAKE A LARGE BOWL, CRACK EGGS AND WHISK IT WELL. ADD-IN PARMESAN CHEESE, GARLIC POWDER, ALMOND FLOUR, SALT, AND CAYENNE PEPPER, STIR IT GENTLY UNTIL ALL THE INGREDIENTS ARE COMBINED
- TAKE A NON-STICK FRYING PAN TO ADD COCONUT OIL AND LEAVE IT TO HOT OVER MEDIUM HEAT. SCOOP BATTER GENEROUSLY IN THE PAN AND FLATTEN IT BY USING A SPOON. MAKE SURE THE THICKNESS IS ABOUT ½ INCHES. COOK FOR ABOUT 3-5 MINUTES, THEN FLIP THE SIDES TO COOK FOR ANOTHER 5 MINUTES UNTIL IT IS GOLDEN BROWN.
- REPEAT THE PROCESS WITH LEFT BATTER
- SERVE WITH SRIRACHA SAUCE AND ENJOY IT WITH YOUR FRIENDS!

CHOCOLATE PUDDING

SERVING: 2 PERSONS
COOKING TIME: 15 MIN

CARBS: 133G
PROTEIN: 21G
FATS: 174G
FIBER: 4.1G
SODIUM: 326MG
CALORIES: 2150 KCAL

INGREDIENTS

- 2 CUPS HEAVY CREAM
- 1 ½ TSP GELATIN POWDER
- ½ CUP GRANULATED SUGAR
- ⅓ CUP ERYTHRITOL
- ¼ CUP COCOA POWDER
- ¼ KOSHER SALT
- 1 TSP VANILLA EXTRACT

INSTRUCTIONS

- TAKE A SMALL BOWL AND POUR HEAVY CREAM INTO IT
- SPRINKLE GELATIN POWDER OVER IT AND WHISK IT GENTLY
- TAKE A MEDIUM PAN AND LET IT HOT OVER MEDIUM HEAT. ADD-IN CREAM, SUGAR, COCOA POWDER, AND KOSHER SALT. WHISK IT CONTINUOUSLY FOR 5 MINUTES UNTIL IT BECOMES A SMOOTH MIXTURE AND BUBBLES BEGINS TO RISE
- TURN OFF THE HEAT AND ADD VANILLA EXTRACT AND STIR IT THEN ADD GELATIN
- CONTINUE STIRRING UNTIL IT BECOMES A SMOOTH MIXTURE.
- LET IT COOL FOR 10 MINUTES. POUR IN A GLASS AND REFRIGERATE IT UNTIL FIRM. ENJOY YOUR DAY!

ALMOND BUTTER COOKIES

SERVING: 4 PERSONS
COOKING TIME: 25 MIN

CARBS: 38G
PROTEIN: 57G
FATS: 142G
FIBER: 26G
SODIUM: 73MG
CALORIES: 1982KCAL

INGREDIENTS

- 1 CUP ALMOND BUTTER
- 1 SMALL EGG
- ½ CUP ZERO CARB SWEETENER
- ½ TSP VANILLA EXTRACT

INSTRUCTIONS

- PREHEAT THE OVEN AND LINE A PARCHMENT PAPER IN A BAKING TRAY
- COMBINE ALMOND BUTTER, EGG, VANILLA, AND SUGAR AND BLEND IT WELL.
- SPRAY YOUR HANDS WITH OLIVE OIL SO THE DOUGH MAY NOT GET STICKY. PINCH FORK IN THE DOUGH AND SHAPE 12 SIZED BALLS
- NOW MOVE THE DOUGH TO A COOKIE SHEET AND PLACE PARCHMENT PAPER IN IT.
- BAKE COOKIES AT 250°F FOR 20 MINUTES AND FINALLY SERVE IT!

PEANUT MUFFINS

SERVING: 4 PERSONS
COOKING TIME: 25 MIN

CARBS: 128G
PROTEIN: 66G
FATS: 113G
FIBER: 16G
SODIUM: 2501MG
CALORIES: 2140 KCAL

INGREDIENTS

- 1 ¼ CUP PEANUT FLOUR
- ½ CUP MELTED BUTTER
- 3 LARGE EGGS
- 1 TSP BAKING SODA
- ¾ CUP ZERO CARB SUGAR
- ¼ CUP COCONUT FLOUR

INSTRUCTIONS

- PREHEAT THE OVEN TO 350°F.
- TAKE A BOWL AND ADD PEANUT FLOUR, BUTTER, EGGS, BAKING SODA, SUGAR, AND COCONUT FLOUR.
- MIX ALL THE INGREDIENTS WELL AND CONTINUE MIXING UNTIL IT GETS COMBINED.
- POUR MUFFINS INTO A PAN AND BAKE FOR 15-20 MINUTES UNTIL THE COLOR GETS BROWN.
- SERVE IT WITH TEA!

Manufactured by Amazon.ca
Bolton, ON